REVISE GCSE (9–1)
Spelling, Punctuation and Grammar

For English Language and Literature, Humanities, Religious Studies and Science

REVISION GUIDE

Author: Giles Clare

Also available to support your revision:

Revise GCSE Study Skills Guide   9781447967071

The **Revise GCSE Study Skills Guide** is full of tried-and-trusted hints and tips for how to learn more effectively. It gives you techniques to help you achieve your best – throughout your GCSE studies and beyond!

REVISE GCSE
Study Skills
GUIDE

Revise GCSE Revision Planner   9781447967828

The **Revise GCSE Revision Planner** helps you to plan and organise your time, step-by-step, throughout your GCSE revision. Use this book and wall chart to mastermind your revision.

REVISE GCSE
REVISION PLANNER

> **For the full range of Pearson revision titles across KS2, KS3, GCSE, Functional Skills, AS/A Level and BTEC visit:**
> www.pearsonschools.co.uk/revise

When SPaG counts

In some subjects, marks are awarded especially for spelling, punctuation, grammar and specialist terminology. This is a good opportunity to gain extra marks.

How many SPaG marks are awarded in the subjects I study?

The number of SPaG marks will vary by exam board. However, all of the exam boards will make the same **percentage** of marks available for SPaG.

English Language	20%	In English Language, SPaG has its own assessment objective (AO6). This means that strong spelling, punctuation and grammar are worth one fifth of the marks in this exam. The exact wording of AO6 is *Candidates must use a range of vocabulary and sentence structures for clarity, purpose and effect, with accurate spelling and punctuation.*
English Literature	5%	In English Literature, SPaG has its own assessment objective (AO4). The exact wording of AO4 is *Use a range of vocabulary and sentence structures for clarity, purpose and effect, with accurate spelling and punctuation.*
History, Geography, Religious Studies	5%	To get high SPaG marks, you need to be able to... • *spell and punctuate with consistent accuracy* • *use rules of grammar with effective control of meaning overall* • *use a wide range of specialist terms as appropriate.*
Biology, Chemistry, Physics	0%	Science doesn't have a SPaG mark allocation. However, to score highly in extended answers in Science, you need to be able to make your point clearly and coherently, and to link your ideas together effectively. One of the best ways to do this is through good spelling, punctuation and grammar – and especially by using effective sentence structures.

How will I know which questions carry SPaG marks?

SPaG marks are awarded for using a range of suitable vocabulary and sentence structures, accurate spelling and punctuation, and terminology relevant to the subject.

You won't get SPaG marks for every question on a paper so make sure you know when SPaG counts. Questions with SPaG marks will often be indicated in one of the following ways:

• asterisks (*), e.g. in Edexcel Geography A, you'll see * next to the question text and a note in bold at the top of the page

• brackets, e.g. in AQA English Literature, you'll see **AO4 [4 marks]** under the total marks for a question

• symbols, e.g. in OCR History A, you'll see (✏) **Spelling, punctuation and grammar and the use of specialist terminology [5]** under the total marks for a question.

Check with your teacher what to look out for in your exams.

Contents

Standard English

In all your exams, it is important to use **Standard English**. This is a form of grammatically correct English that avoids the use of informal language, as well as slang and dialect words.

Don't write how you speak

Most people don't exclusively use Standard English in everyday conversations. Here are some examples of what people sometimes say and what you should write instead:

Spoken English (non-Standard)	Written English (Standard)
I ain't revised for this exam.	I haven't revised for this exam.
He done good in his test.	He did well in his test.
Me and my mate didn't see nothing.	My friend and I didn't see anything.
You could of told me, like.	You could have told me, couldn't you?
She been in trouble with the fuzz.	She has been in trouble with the police.

Contractions

Contractions are acceptable in Standard English. However, to make your writing more suitable for answering exam questions, you should avoid such contractions. There are two exceptions to this rule. First, if you are quoting directly from a source, make sure you write out any contractions exactly as they appear. Second, you may choose to use contractions in your creative writing to make speech more natural.

Slang and dialect

Words like **mate** and phrases like **the fuzz** in the table above are examples of **slang**. Slang is widely-used, informal language that is not Standard English. You should avoid using slang words in your exam answers.

Dialect refers to certain non-Standard words and expressions that are used by people in a particular region. Cockney rhyming slang is an example dialectal language. You should avoid using dialect words in formal writing.

slang   slang contraction   non-Standard English

Some people are well gutted cos they ain't allowed to practise their religions in them countries. ✗

Some people are deeply upset because they are not allowed to practise their religions in those countries. ✓

This is better as the writer has used Standard English throughout.

Now try this

Rewrite these sentences in Standard English.
- (a)   There ain't no excuse for messin up the environment for the kids in the future.
- (b)   The main character of dis novel don't seem like a pucker gent.
- (c)   Macbeth shouldn't of bumped off his mate, King Duncan.

Formal & informal language

We express ourselves in different registers when we speak and write, according to the context of the interaction. There are two registers: **formal** and **informal**.

Audience and purpose

Before writing, make sure you have a clear idea of who you are writing for (the audience) and what you are trying to say (the purpose). These examples have the same purpose (asking someone to send something) but different audiences.

This informal example is more suited to communicating casually with a close friend or colleague:

slang words   casual vocabulary   abbreviations

> Hi mate, do me a fave. Fork out for some new sports stuff asap. Ta.

This formal example is more appropriate for writing politely to a stranger:

formal expressions   precise technical vocabulary

> Dear Sir, I am writing to request that you subsidise the provision of some new sports equipment at your earliest convenience. Thank you.

Answering exam questions

Things to avoid:

✗ Co-ordinating conjunctions (**and, but, or**) at the start of a sentence, unless it is for effect in narrative or transactional writing

✗ Imprecise slang vocabulary (**nice, sort of**)

✗ Casual discourse markers (**like I just said**)

✗ Text message-style punctuation (**!!!**) and abbreviations (**lol**)

Things to include:

✓ Subordinating conjunctions at the start of a complex sentence (**although, however**)

✓ Precise vocabulary (**investigate, require**)

✓ Formal conjunctions (**first, nevertheless**)

✓ A range of punctuation (**colons, dashes**)

Getting it right

In general, you should use formal language in your exam, unless informal language is required by the audience or the genre.

Look through your work and make a list of the precise vocabulary you use regularly. Practise spelling these words to make sure you get them right in your exams.

Now try this

1 Rewrite these phrases to make them more suitable for an exam answer: I wanna chat about; I wanna get on with; I reckon it's proper uncool that.

2 Rewrite this sentence in a more formal register.
   Right now, it looks like what them politics guys decided is gonna screw up the economy.

Double letters

A **suffix** is a group of letters added to the end of a root word. When you add a suffix, you sometimes need to **double** the final letter of the root word. There are two main rules for when to do this.

Adding a suffix to a Consonant–Vowel–Consonant (CVC) root

If a one-syllable root word ends in a CVC pattern, double the final consonant before you add the suffix.

't' is a consonant (C).   'o' is a vowel (V).   'p' is a consonant (C).

> A root word is a word without a prefix or a suffix already attached to it.

Double the 'p' when you add the suffix.

stop → stopping

Here are some other examples:

| rub | → | rubber | plan | → | planned |
| wed | → | wedding | put | → | putting |

Syllable stress

If the root word has more than one syllable, decide which syllable is stressed.

If the stress falls on the first (or penultimate) syllable ('vis'), do not double the final consonant ('t').

visit → visitor

If the stress falls on the last syllable ('gin'), double the final consonant ('n').

begin → beginning

Here are some other examples:

| finish | → | finished | refer | → | referral |
| answer | → | answering | omit | → | omitted |

These rules only apply if the first letter of the suffix is a vowel. For example, **sad** can become **sadden** (CVC rule plus vowel), but **sad** can also become **sadly** (no double 'd' because **-ly** doesn't start with a vowel).

To revise the spelling rules for other types of suffixes, see pages 10–11.

Now try this

1 Write down these verbs and underline the syllable that is stressed in each one: export; travel; complain; elect; straighten.
2 Which of these underlined words are spelled correctly? he joged; an openning; they entered; calculators are permitted; she admited.
3 Correct the incorrect words in Question 2.

> If you're not sure, say the word out loud, first with stress on the first syllable, then with stress on the second syllable. Which sounds right?

Silent letters

Some words are tricky to spell because they contain letters that are not sounded out when you say them.

Silent consonants

Some consonants are **not pronounced** at all in certain words. Here are some examples:

Silent b	Silent c	Silent g	Silent h	Silent k
debt	science	sign	honest	knife
climb	muscle	align	ghetto	knowledge
doubt	scissors	foreign	rhyme	knight
subtle	descend	campaign	exhibition	knuckle
limb	disciples	sovereign	chemistry	knoll

Silent l	Silent n	Silent t	Silent w	Silent s
calm	autumn	fasten	answer	island
should	condemn	castle	wrong	debris
chalk	hymn	mortgage	write	aisle
half	solemn	apostles	whole	bourgeois
could	column	tsar	two	islet

Unstressed vowels

Some words have unstressed vowels, which means that they are not sounded out clearly when we say them. Here are some examples:

Unstressed a	Unstressed e	Unstressed i	Unstressed o	Unstressed u
library	difference	medicine	factory	guess
parliament	generally	definitely	category	tongue
dictionary	desperate	easily	colonel	guitar
boundary	frightening	business	people	colleague
separate	interesting	sovereign	leopard	guard

Spelling vowel sounds

Watch out for words with vowels that may sound like other vowels, for example, **secret, language** and **among**. Vowels can also sound different in certain words due to the accent of the speaker. Make sure you learn the correct spellings.

Now try this

1 Write down these words and underline the silent letters: salmon; rhythm; indictment; ballet; wrist.

2 Write down these words, filling in the missing silent letters: _not; s_ord; thum_; whis_le; ca_ves; _onour.

3 Write down these words, filling in the missing unstressed vowels or correcting the one that is underlined: veg_tables; discription; calender; nec_ssary; g_sthouse.

Plurals: adding -s and -es

A **plural noun** is a word that identifies more than one of the same thing. There are a few different ways of writing plural nouns. Look at the final letters of the singular noun to help you decide how to write the correct plural ending.

Adding -s

Most of the time, you simply add **-s** to the end of a singular noun to make it plural. Here are some examples:

car	→	cars	house	→ houses
subject	→	subjects	pencil	→ pencils
adjective	→	adjectives	fountain	→ fountains
poem	→	poems	language	→ languages
animal	→	animals	frustration	→ frustrations

Adding -es

For some nouns, you need to add **-es** instead of just -s to make it plural. These nouns end with 's', 'x', 'z', 'ch' and 'sh'. Here are some examples:

> Never add apostrophe 's' to make a noun plural. Apostrophes are only used to show possession or where letters are missing.

See pages 36–37 for more on apostrophes.

s	virus	→	viruses	compass	→	compasses
x	prefix	→	prefixes	tax	→	taxes
z	buzz	→	buzzes	waltz	→	waltzes
ch	arch	→	arches	sketch	→	sketches
sh	wish	→	wishes	crash	→	crashes

> Words that need **-es** would be hard to say if you just added -s. For example, try saying **compasss**.

Golden rule

Add **-es** if the singular noun ends in 's', 'x', 'z', 'ch' or 'sh'.

Now try this

1 Write the plural form of these nouns: process; landscape; knight; ecosystem; box; business; bias; dish; minus; complex.

2 Write the singular form of these nouns: eyelashes; synonyms; prospectuses; quizzes; phrases; fishes; guides; churches; mixes; equinoxes.

3 Rewrite this sentence, correcting the plurals.
The pupiles sat on the benchs while the teacheres sorted out their classs.

4 Rewrite this sentence, making all of the nouns plural.
The painter put the brush into the jar, and examined the atlas and the sketch.

> **Quizzes** follows the add **-es** rule, but also needs a spelling change.

Plurals: words ending in -y

There are many singular nouns that end in **-y**. Fortunately, there are just two straightforward rules you need to know to make them plural.

Vowel before -y

If the **-y** follows a vowel, you add **-s**. Here are some examples:

essay → essays	screenplay → screenplays	delay → delays
convoy → convoys	causeway → causeways	tray → trays
key → keys	alley → alleys	quay → quays
storey → storeys	journey → journeys	abbey → abbeys
valley → valleys	kidney → kidneys	array → arrays

The **-y** follows a vowel (in this case an 'e'), so you add **-s** to make the plural form.

The **-y** follows a consonant (in this case an 'm'), so you drop the **-y** and add **-ies** to make the plural form.

Consonant before -y

If the **-y** follows a consonant, you drop the **-y** and add **-ies**.

ally → allies	colony → colonies	army → armies
city → cities	academy → academies	history → histories
navy → navies	technology → technologies	enemy → enemies
victory → victories	university → universities	ability → abilities
allergy → allergies	country → countries	study → studies

Now try this

1 Copy this table and add the nouns under the correct heading.

Vowel before -y	Consonant before -y

    clergy   century   attorney   necessity   decoy

    galley   prophecy   holiday   deity   survey

2 Rewrite each noun in the table in the plural form, using the correct spelling rule.

Plurals: other endings

There are also rules for the plurals of nouns ending in letters other than **-y**, such as **-o**, **-f** and **-fe**. However, you should watch out for exceptions to these rules.

Nouns ending in -o

As a general rule, you should **simply add -s** to the end of a singular noun ending in **-o** to make it plural, but there are also some exceptions. Here are some examples:

Add -s		
cello	→	cellos
portfolio	→	portfolios
zoo	→	zoos
inferno	→	infernos
video	→	videos

Add -es		
potato	→	potatoes
embargo	→	embargoes
veto	→	vetoes
volcano	→	volcanoes
echo	→	echoes

Can be spelled either way		
tornado	→	tornado(e)s
mango	→	mango(e)s
ghetto	→	ghetto(e)s
cargo	→	cargo(e)s
flamingo	→	flamingo(e)s

There's no easy way to remember which nouns follow the rule. However, where there is a vowel directly before the final **-o**, you always add just **-s**.

Nouns ending in -f or -fe

There are two main rules for making these words plural: either change the **-f** to **-v** and add **-es**, or keep the **-f** and add **-s**. Here are some examples:

Change -f to -v, add -es		
knife	→	knives
loaf	→	loaves
half	→	halves
wife	→	wives
elf	→	elves

Keep -f, add -s		
proof	→	proofs
reef	→	reefs
spoof	→	spoofs
chief	→	chiefs
belief	→	beliefs

Exceptions to both rules		
gulf	→	gulfs
chef	→	chefs
safe	→	safes
wharf	→	wharfs or wharves
hoof	→	hoofs or hooves

All of these nouns end in two vowels plus **-f**. They form the plural by adding **-s**.

Now try this

1 Write the plural form of these nouns: leaf; self; debrief; wolf; roof.
2 Rewrite these sentences, correcting the plurals.
  (a) The wifes took some knifes off the shelfs and put them in the saves due to their believes about safety.
  (b) I saw some elfs on the rooves, running for their lives from some wolfs.

Irregular plurals

Some nouns have an **irregular** plural form, which means they don't follow the rules covered on pages 5–7.

Unmarked plurals

Some nouns don't change in the plural form. These are called unmarked plurals.
Examples include some animals, especially types of fish:

You can also say fishes but it's much less common.

| deer | fish | moose | sheep | trout | cod | shrimp |

Other nouns that don't change when made plural include the following:

You can also say **cannons**.

| species | spacecraft | offspring | series | cannon |

Other common irregular plurals

Some nouns have an irregular form in the plural. Many of these are left over from Old English or come from Greek. Here are some examples:

child	→	children	criterion	→	criteria
man	→	men	hypothesis	→	hypotheses
die	→	dice	index	→	indices
person	→	people	matrix	→	matrices
foot	→	feet	datum	→	data
tooth	→	teeth	analysis	→	analyses
mouse	→	mice	genus	→	genera
radius	→	radii	parenthesis	→	parentheses

There is no golden rule for these spellings, so you will need to learn how to spell each plural word individually. Saying the words aloud will help you to match the plural forms to their spellings.

Index has an alternative plural.
Indexes is also correct.

Notice that many of these words will be useful in your exams.

Now try this

1 Rewrite this sentence, correcting the plurals.
His hypothesises were based on analysises of fish genuses and observation of salmons in their natural habitat.

2 Rewrite this sentence, making sure all of the plurals are correct.
All person should chase the goose, sheep and ox out of the three aircraft.

Prefixes

A **prefix** is a group of letters added to the front of a root word. It does not make sense on its own.

Negative or opposite meaning

When you add a prefix to a root word, you **change the meaning.** Prefixes often create negatives or opposites of their root word. Here are some examples:

un-	unhappy, unintended, unconstitutional, unnecessary, unable, unzip
im-	impossible, immoral, imprecise, immeasurable, impatient, imbalance
in-	inaccurate, inefficient, invisible, incomplete, informal, inactive, invalidate
mis-	misfortune, misdirection, mismanage, misrule, misleading, mismanagement
dis-	disobey, dissent, discover, disappearance, disqualify, dishonesty, disown
ir-	irrelevant, irregular, irresponsible, irreligious, irrevocable
il-	illegal, illogical, illegible, illiberal
a-/an-	amoral, asexual, agnostic, atonal, amorphous, anaesthetic, anaerobic
de-	dehydrated, deregulation, detoxify, destructive, declassify, desalination
non-	nonsense, nonentity, nonpartisan, nonreligious, nonconformist
mal-	maladjusted, malcontent, malnutrition, malpractice
anti-	antisocial, anticlockwise, anticoagulant, antibiotics

Different meanings

Other prefixes give the root word a different meaning, depending on the prefix used. Here are some examples:

aero-	aeronautics, aeroplane, aerodynamics
eco-	ecosystem, ecology, economy, ecotourism
inter-	international, interstate, intervention, interaction
bi-	bicycle, bilingual, biannually, bigamy, bipedal
mega-	megacity, megaphone, megabyte, megahertz
pre-	predict, precede, prenatal, preeclampsia, prefix
sub-	submarine, subset, subway, subsonic, subtitles

The prefix **pre-** means **before.** The word **predict** means to guess what might happen **before** it takes place.

Golden rule

You never have to change the spelling of the root word when you add a prefix.
You simply add the prefix to the front of the root word.

Now try this

1   Add the correct prefix to each of these words to give it a negative or opposite meaning: loyal; perfection; stop; nourished; realistic; literate; compatible; reversible; diagnosis; code; aerobic.

2   Look up and learn a new word beginning with each of the prefixes listed above. Try to find words related to the subjects you are studying.

Suffixes: changes to word endings

A **suffix** is a group of letters added to the end of a **root word**. Just like adding a prefix, adding a suffix can change the meaning of the root word.

Word ending changes

When you add a suffix, you often need to change the spelling of the end of the root word. The table below shows the general spelling rules you should follow:

Root word ends with...	Suffix	Rule	Example
a **vowel**.	begins with a consonant	Keep the 'e'.	clue + **less** → clueless
a **vowel**.	begins with a vowel	Drop the 'e'.	pure + **ify** → purify
a **vowel and a 'y'**.	any suffix	Keep the 'y'.	employ + **ee** → employee
a **consonant and a 'y'**.	any suffix, except -ing	Change the 'y' to an 'i'.	mercy + **ful** → merciful
a **consonant and a 'y'**.	-ing	Keep the 'y'.	marry + **ing** → marrying
'ie'.	-ing	Change the 'ie' to a 'y'.	lie + **ing** → lying

Most suffixes do not make sense on their own. Two exceptions are **-able** and **-less**.

To revise when you need to use double letters, see page 3.

To revise the rules for plurals, see pages 5–8.

Now try this

1 Identify the correct spelling in each of these pairs:

   (a) theories / theorys   (b) praied / prayed   (c) envyous / envious

   (d) securly / securely   (e) tieing / tying

2 Add the suffixes to these root words:

   (a) beauty + ful   (b) die + ing   (c) approximate + ly

   (d) valley + s   (e) study + ed

Check which rule applies to each of these examples before you decide on your answers.

Suffixes: adding to root words

You can add **suffixes** to a **root word** to make new words, such as nouns, adjectives, verbs and adverbs. Suffixes can also change the tense of verbs.

Word types

Adding different suffixes to a root creates different types of words.
Here is an example:

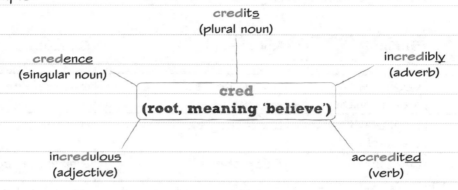

credit**s**
(plural noun)

cred**ence**
(singular noun)

in**cred**ibl**y**
(adverb)

cred
(root, meaning 'believe')

incredul**ous**
(adjective)

ac**cred**it**ed**
(verb)

Tricky endings

Some suffix endings sound the same as or very similar to each other. You will need to learn the following spellings as well as any other examples you come across:

-tion	ambition, revolution, solution, nation, pollution, introduction
-sion	decision, recession, conclusion, discussion, profession, exclusion
-cian	politician, musician, technician, patrician, optician
-cion	suspicion, coercion
-tious	cautious, infectious, nutritious, superstitious, fictitious
-cious	conscious, precious, suspicious, vicious, malicious
-tial	potential, essential, residential, initial, partial, influential
-cial	antisocial, official, commercial, racial, beneficial, glacial
-able	available, variable, suitable, capable, vegetable, syllable
-ible	possible, visible, flexible, accessible, audible, irreversible
-ent	government, development, management, president, environment
-ant	significant, defendant, relevant, peasant, merchant, protestant
-ence	experience, evidence, difference, science, conference, consequence
-ance	performance, importance, finance, insurance, distance, alliance

Now try this

1 Correct the spelling of each of these words by changing the suffix: creacion; negligance; absorbant; preventible; marcial; pretencious.

2 Look up and learn a new word ending in each of the suffixes listed above. Try to find words related to the subject(s) you are studying.

Homophones: contractions

A **homophone** is a word that sounds like another word but is spelled differently and has a different meaning.

Your and you're

contraction of **you are**   possessive pronoun (the mistake belonging to you)

You're trying to blame me for **your** mistake.

Apostrophes are often used to show where a letter or letters have been removed when two words are joined together. Such words are known as **contractions**.

For more information on contractions, see page 35.

To revise how to use apostrophes correctly, see pages 36–37.

It's and its

contraction of **it is**

It's an example of metamorphic rock.

possessive pronoun (the banks belong to the river)

The river overflowed **its** banks.

There, their and they're

shows place or position   possessive pronoun (the army belongs to them)

There were many casualties. **Their** army was decimated. **They're** retreating.

contraction of **they are**

Now try this

1 Write out each sentence, using the correct homophone from the word bank on the right.

(a) Why is _____ so much traffic today?

(b) Germany was forced to pay reparations to _____ neighbours.

(c) Please call if you have not received _____ parcel.

your	you're	their
there	its	it's

2 Rewrite these sentences, replacing the underlined words with the correct homophones.

(a) <u>Their</u> is no evidence for <u>you're</u> argument.

(b) The dog thinks <u>its</u> time for <u>it's</u> tea.

(c) <u>Your</u> not leaving the party before <u>its</u> over.

(d) <u>Its</u> not right that <u>your</u> covering up for <u>there</u> errors.

Homophones: common groups

The groups of words below are common examples of **homophones**. They all sound the same but have different meanings.

To, too and two

indicates a place, direction or position   part of the infinitive verb **to protest**

The group is travelling **to** London. They plan **to** protest outside parliament.

You can put **in** before **to** to make the preposition **into**:
The River Thames flows **into** the North Sea.

adverb meaning **very** or **excessively**   adverb meaning **also**

Dieting is **too** difficult. Getting enough exercise is tricky **too**.

the number 2

The **two** largest religions in the world are Christianity and Islam.

Other common homophones

This table shows common homophone pairs and their different word classes.

Homophone pairs	Examples
here	How far is it from **here** to Cardiff? (indicates position)
hear	The soldiers could not **hear** the orders. (verb)
past	The train rushed **past** the station without stopping. (indicates direction)
passed	The policewoman **passed** her fitness test. (verb in the past tense)
allowed	The Normans **allowed** some slaves to go free. (verb in the past tense)
aloud	Read all these words **aloud**. (adverb meaning **spoken out loud**)
which	**Which** is the largest city in Europe? (question word)
witch	Hecate is the lead **witch** in Macbeth. (noun)
where	**Where** is chalk found in Britain? (question word)
wear	Sikh men usually **wear** a turban to cover their hair. (verb)
practice	The school carried out a fire **practice**. (noun)
practise	The majority of people in India **practise** Hinduism. (verb)
licence	Companies require a **licence** to emit greenhouse gases. (noun)
license	MI6 can **license** a secret agent to kill. (verb)

Now try this

1 Write down the correct homophone to complete each of these sentences.

(a) What are the indirect threats *too* / *to* the taiga biome?

(b) The geld tax *allowed* / *aloud* William to collect money from his kingdom.

2 Use the word bank on the right to fill in the gaps with the correct homophones.

(a) _____ did Macbeth and Banquo meet the three _____?

(b) She _____ her driving test and now she has her _____.

(c) In _____ room can I _____ reading my _____ speeches _____?

practice	practise
where	wear
licence	license
whichs	witches
witch	which
allowed	aloud
passed	past

Common spelling errors

Some words **sound very similar** but have different spellings and meanings. Other words **look similar** but sound different and have different meanings.

Near homophones

Words that sound almost the same but have different spellings and meanings are **near homophones**.

Near homophones	Examples
our	It was **our** mistake to leave early. (possessive pronoun)
are	We **are** going to regret making that mistake. (part of the verb **to be**)
off	The diver jumped **off** the tall cliff. (preposition)
of	Deforestation pushes animals out **of** their habitats. (preposition)
advise	Lord Melbourne used to **advise** Queen Victoria. (verb)
advice	The boy did not take the **advice** he was given. (noun)
devise	The scientists had to **devise** a method for testing their theory. (verb)
device	An anemometer is a **device** for measuring wind speed. (noun)
quiet	Jungles are not usually **quiet** places at night. (adjective)
quite	A terrier is **quite** small compared to other dogs. (adverb meaning **fairly**)
accept	Atheists do not **accept** the existence of deities. (verb)
except	Most major religions worship gods, **except** Buddhism. (preposition)
precede	The Anglo-Saxons **preceded** the Normans. (verb meaning **came before**)
proceed	The Allies **proceeded** with the invasion. (verb meaning **went ahead with**)
lose	The workers did not want to **lose** their rights. (verb)
loose	There was a **loose** bull in the field. (adjective)

Other common errors

The words in each pair below look very similar but sound different and have different meanings:

Words that look similar	Examples
bought	The football team **bought** a new player. (past tense of verb 'to buy')
brought	Moses **brought** the Israelites out of Egypt. (past tense of verb **to bring**)
though	Even **though** he was ill, he worked every day. (meaning **despite the fact that**)
thought	She **thought** it was time to revise. (past tense of verb **to think**)
through	The advance broke **through** the enemy lines. (preposition)
thorough	You need a **thorough** understanding of the subject. (meaning **in depth**)

Now try this

Rewrite these sentences, replacing the underlined words with the correct words.

(a) On your <u>advise</u>, I <u>brought</u> a watch <u>of</u> the internet. I hope I won't <u>loose</u> it.

(b) A lot <u>off</u> <u>are</u> employees are expressing their <u>descent</u> in the streets.

(c) Engineers have made a <u>through</u> examination of the <u>devise</u> and they <u>advice</u> that it is now safe.

(d) Even <u>thought</u> the room was <u>quite</u>, everyone was awake <u>accept</u> George.

14

'i' before 'e'

The letter strings '**ie**' and '**ei**' are very common in English. It is sometimes tricky to know which one to use.

When the sound is 'ee', 'i' before 'e' except after 'c'

In most cases when using these two letters, you should put the 'i' before the 'e'. However, this can change when they directly follow a 'c' and the sound they make is **ee**.

The 'i' comes before the 'e' because it follows 'ch' (not just 'c').

| believe | chief | brief | piece | diesel |

Notice that all of the 'ie' and 'ei' letter strings in these words make the sound **ee**.

The 'e' comes before the 'i' because it follows 'c'.

| ceiling | perceive | receipt | deceive | conceit |

Exceptions to the rule

There are some words in which the 'ei' letter string makes the **ee** sound but doesn't follow a 'c'. You will need to learn these exceptions. Here are some examples:

'ei' is used even though it follows 't' not 'c'.

| seize | caffeine | protein |

When the rule doesn't apply

If the 'ie' or 'ei' letter string doesn't make the sound **ee**, the 'i' before 'e' except after 'c' rule doesn't apply. Here are some examples you will need to learn:

'ie' doesn't make an **ee** sound.   'ei' doesn't make an **ee** sound.

| science | efficient | foreign | weight |

Getting it right

Mostly, 'i' comes before 'e' except after 'c' when the sound is **ee**. You should learn the exceptions.

Now try this

1   Write down these words, inserting the correct letter string ('ie' or 'ei') in the gaps: th__f; rec__ve; f__ld; decaff__nated; conc__ve.

2   Correct the spelling of each of these words: beleif; nieghbour; decietful; biege; preist; feirce; liesure.

Say the words out loud. Which contain the **ee** sound and which don't?

Spellings for GCSE History

It is easy to misspell certain words that you may need in your History exams.

Tricky spellings

It will be useful to learn to spell the following words correctly. The coloured letters in the left column indicate where people often make spelling mistakes.

Word	Example of use in a sentence
government	The growth of democracy in Germany saw the exchanging of power from monarchies to parliamentary **government**.
consequence	Some historians argue that Hitler's rise to power was a direct **consequence** of the Versailles Treaty.
interpretation	There are many **interpretations** of the causes of the First World War.
propaganda	**Propaganda** is used to persuade people to agree with a particular political ideal.
persecution	Jim Crow was used as the legal basis for the **persecution** of black people in America.
Roosevelt	Franklin D. **Roosevelt** was the last president to serve more than eight years in office.
inhibited	The strict following of Galenic methods **inhibited** the development of medicine during the medieval period.
contemporary	**Contemporary** historians find new interpretations of historical events.
parliament	The first and second English Civil Wars were fought between supporters of King Charles I and supporters of the Long **Parliament**.
Bolshevik	The **Bolsheviks** came to power during the October Revolution of 1917.
abolitionist	**Abolitionists** fought for the freeing of slaves in Western Europe and the Americas.
Versailles	The Treaty of **Versailles** officially ended the First World War.
suffrage	The Pankhursts were key figures in the women's fight for **suffrage** in the UK.
Mao Tse-tung	**Mao Tse-tung** (Zedong) was the communist leader of the People's Republic of China.

Now try this

1 Identify the words in the table above that you do not know how to spell correctly.

2 Copy this grid and complete the first column by adding your list of words from question 1. Add any other words specific to History you find difficult to spell. Practise each word once a day for a school week, using the **look**, **cover**, **say**, **write**, **check** method.

Word	Monday	Tuesday	Wednesday	Thursday	Friday
government					

First, **look** at the spellings before you **cover** them up. Then, **say** them out loud. Next, **write** them down. Finally, **check** you've spelled them correctly.

16

Spellings for GCSE Geography

It is easy to misspell certain words that you may need in your Geography exams.

Tricky spellings

It will be useful to learn to spell the following words correctly. The coloured letters in the left column indicate where people often make spelling mistakes.

Word	Example of use in a sentence
environment	The construction of major roads may affect the local **environment**.
tectonic	**Tectonic** plates make up the outer shell of the planet.
biome	There are five major **biomes** that make up the ecosystems of the Earth.
interdependence	Globalisation has led to **interdependence** between countries.
hydraulic	**Hydraulic** action breaks up cliff faces by forcing air inside the rock.
reservoir	**Reservoirs** and dams can be used to manage the risk of flooding.
congestion	The massive populations of megacities create large amounts of traffic **congestion**.
cyclone	**Cyclone** Nargis was a category 5 tropical storm.
decentralisation	**Decentralisation** can be found when development takes place outside a central location.
gentrification	**Gentrification** is where poorer areas are developed, causing a rise in living costs and pushing out poorer residents.
igneous	**Igneous** rock is formed from magma.
malnourishment	**Malnourishment** occurs when people do not have ready access to food.
tsunami	When an earthquake happens under the sea, it can cause a **tsunami**.
precipitation	**Precipitation** is high in tropical rainforests.

Now try this

1 Identify the words in the table above that you do not know how to spell correctly.

2 Copy this grid and complete the first column by adding your list of words from question 1. Add any other words specific to Geography that you find difficult to spell. Practise each word once a day for a school week, using the **look**, **cover**, **say**, **write**, **check** method.

Word	Monday	Tuesday	Wednesday	Thursday	Friday
environment					

Spellings for GCSE Religious Studies

It is easy to misspell certain words that you may need in your Religious Studies exams.

Tricky spellings

It will be useful to learn to spell the following words correctly. The coloured letters in the left column indicate where people often make spelling mistakes.

Word	Example of use in a sentence
atheist	An **atheist** is a person who does not believe in the existence of gods.
benevolent	An all-loving God is **benevolent**.
omniscient	An all-knowing God is **omniscient**.
monotheistic	Christianity and Islam are **monotheistic** faiths.
Eucharist	The **Eucharist** is performed at Catholic mass.
synagogue	Jewish people worship at a **synagogue**.
euthanasia	Many religious philosophies disagree with **euthanasia**.
contemporary	**Contemporary** historians often find new interpretations of historical events.
mitzvah	At thirteen, Jewish boys have a **bar mitzvah**, whereas girls have a **bat mitzvah**.
resurrected	Christians believe that Jesus was **resurrected** after the crucifixion.
dharma	**Dharma** is a key concept in many religions and has many meanings and interpretations.
transcendence	Many religions believe in some form of **transcendence** after death.
Qur'an	The Islamic holy book is called the **Qur'an**.
samsara	**Samsara** is the cycle of life and death.
Shi'a	The two main branches of the Islamic faith are Sunni and **Shi'a**.

Now try this

1 Identify the words in the table above that you do not know how to spell correctly.

2 Copy this grid and complete the first column by adding your list of words from question 1. Add any other words specific to Religious Studies that you find difficult to spell. Practise each word once a day for a school week, using the **look**, **cover**, **say**, **write**, **check** method.

Word	Monday	Tuesday	Wednesday	Thursday	Friday
atheist					

Spellings for GCSE Biology

It is easy to misspell certain words that you may need in your Biology exams.

Tricky spellings

It will be useful to learn to spell the following words for your Biology exams. The coloured letters in the left column indicate where people often make spelling mistakes.

Word	Example of use in a sentence
photosynthesis	Plants convert light into energy using the process of **photosynthesis**.
accommodation	**Accommodation** occurs when the lens of your eye changes shape to focus on an object.
alleles	Most genes have two **alleles**: one dominant and one recessive.
diaphragm	The **diaphragm** helps to inflate the lungs during breathing.
endoscope	An **endoscope** uses optical fibres to look inside the body.
electrolysis/ electrolyte	**Electrolysis** takes place in a liquid called an **electrolyte**.
deficiency	If you have a **deficiency**, you are lacking in something.
anaerobic	**Anaerobic** respiration can transfer energy without oxygen.
chlorophyll	Leaves are green because of the presence of **chlorophyll**.
haemoglobin	**Haemoglobin** transports oxygen around the body in the blood.
homozygous/ heterozygous	Someone who is **homozygous** carries two copies of the same allele. Someone who is **heterozygous** carries two different alleles.
plaque	**Plaque** is the name for the build-up of cholesterol in blood vessels.
independent	An **independent** variable is decided upon and changed by the person conducting the experiment.
breathe (verb)/ breath (noun)	When you **breathe**, you inhale and exhale air. The **breath** you exhale contains less oxygen than the **breath** you inhale.
coronary	**Coronary** heart disease is caused by the build-up of fatty acids.

Now try this

1   Identify the words in the table above that you do not know how to spell correctly.

2   Copy this grid and complete the first column by adding your list of words from question 1. Add any other words specific to Biology that you find difficult to spell. Practise each word once a day for a school week, using the **look**, **cover**, **say**, **write**, **check** method.

Word	Monday	Tuesday	Wednesday	Thursday	Friday
photosynthesis					

Spellings for GCSE Chemistry

It is easy to misspell certain words that you may need in your Chemistry exams.

Tricky spellings

It will be useful to learn to spell the following words correctly. The coloured letters in the left column indicate where people often make spelling mistakes.

Word	Example of use in a sentence
aqueous	An **aqueous** solution uses water as a solvent.
decolourised	When a coloured solution becomes colourless, we say it has **decolourised**.
chromatography	**Chromatography** separates the components of a chemical mixture.
covalent	**Covalent** bonds are formed when atoms share a pair of electrons.
buckminsterfullerene	**Buckminsterfullerene** contains 60 carbon atoms in the shape of a ball.
crystallography	**Crystallography** describes the structure of a crystal, usually through the use of X-ray diffraction.
Avogadro	The **Avogadro** constant states the number of atoms, molecules or ions in a mole of any given substance (6.02×10^{23}).
magnesium	**Magnesium** is a group two element with the chemical symbol Mg.
reversible	If a **reversible** reaction is endothermic in one direction, it will be exothermic in the other.
catalyst	Iron is used as a **catalyst** in the production of ammonia.
meiosis	**Meiosis** is a type of cell division that produces four daughter cells.
equilibrium	**Equilibrium** occurs in a closed system when the rates of the forward and reverse reactions are equal.
Le Chatelier's	If a change is made to a system at equilibrium, **Le Chatelier's** principle states that the system will work to counteract the change.
viscosity	**Viscosity** in hydrocarbons increases with molecular weight.
homologous	Ethene, propene and butene are the first three members of the **homologous** series of alkenes.

Now try this

1 Identify the words in the table above that you do not know how to spell correctly.

2 Copy this grid and complete the first column by adding your list of words from question 1. Add any other words specific to Chemistry you find difficult to spell. Practise each word once a day for a school week, using the **look**, **cover**, **say**, **write**, **check** method.

Word	Monday	Tuesday	Wednesday	Thursday	Friday
aqueous					

Spellings for GCSE Physics

It is easy to misspell certain words that you may need in your Physics exams.

Tricky spellings

It will be useful to learn to spell the following words correctly. The coloured letters in the left column indicate where people often make spelling mistakes.

Word	Example of use in a sentence
seismic	**Seismic** waves can be caused by rock breaking in the earth or by an explosion.
nuclear fission	**Nuclear fission** is the process of splitting a nucleus to form two or more nuclei of smaller atomic number.
emission	The **emission** of greenhouse gases has led to a net increase in global temperature.
inertia	**Inertia** is the innate tendency for an object to resist changes in velocity.
velocity	**Velocity** measures the speed of a moving object in a given direction.
neutron	There are no **neutrons** in a hydrogen atom.
efficiency	**Efficiency** is improved in maglev trains by reducing the energy wasted through friction.
satellite	Earth's moon is a natural **satellite**.
oscilloscope	An **oscilloscope** can be used to measure the change in an electrical signal over time.
coulomb	The SI unit for measuring electrical charge is the **coulomb**, C.
anomaly	An **anomaly** is a measurement that exists far outside the expected or observed trend.
dissipated	The more energy **dissipated** from an engine, the lower the efficiency.
longitudinal	**Longitudinal** waves occur parallel to the direction of energy transfer.
infrared	**Infrared** light has a lower wavelength than that of visible light.
translucent	A **translucent** object will transmit light but, due to diffraction through the material, cannot be seen through clearly.

Now try this

1 Identify the words in the table above that you do not know how to spell correctly.

2 Copy this grid and complete the first column by adding your list of words from question 1. Add any other words specific to Physics you find difficult to spell. Practise each word once a day for a school week, using the **look**, **cover**, **say**, **write**, **check** method.

Word	Monday	Tuesday	Wednesday	Thursday	Friday
seismic					

Spellings for GCSE English Literature

It is easy to misspell certain words that you may need in your English Literature exams. You will be expected to know how to spell them correctly.

Tricky spellings

It will be useful to learn to spell the following words correctly. The coloured letters in the left column indicate where people often make spelling mistakes.

Word	Example of use in a sentence
soliloquy	A **soliloquy** is a dramatic monologue in which the character talks aloud to himself or herself.
allegorical	Animal farm is an **allegorical** novel.
iambic pentameter	A sonnet is a 14-line poem written in **iambic pentameter**.
metaphor	A **metaphor** directly compares one thing to another to build a more abstract image.
rhyme	Poetry doesn't have to **rhyme**.
rhythm	**Rhythm** is the pattern of stressed and unstressed syllables within a line of verse.
onomatopoeia	**Onomatopoeia** refers to words that sound like what they describe.
stanza	A **stanza** is a group of lines in a poem with a line break before and after.
anthropomorphism	**Anthropomorphism** is the technique of giving human characteristics to animals.
euphemism	A **euphemism** is an indirect expression used to refer to something embarrassing or unpleasant.
dialogue	**Dialogue** is speech carried out between two or more characters.
pathetic fallacy	**Pathetic fallacy** is the technique of attributing an emotion or mood to a natural phenomenon.
enjambment	The poet uses **enjambment** to mimic the urgency of the event.

Now try this

1 Identify the words in the table above that you do not know how to spell correctly.

2 Copy this grid and complete the first column by adding your list of words from question 1. Add any other Words specific to English Literature that you find difficult to spell. Practise each word once a day for a school week, using the **look**, **cover**, **say**, **write**, **check** method.

Word	Monday	Tuesday	Wednesday	Thursday	Friday
soliloquy					

Spellings for GCSE English Language

It is easy to misspell certain words that you may need in your English Language exams. You will be expected to know how to spell them correctly.

Tricky spellings

It will be useful to learn to spell the following words correctly. The coloured letters in the left column indicate where people often make spelling mistakes.

Word	Example of use in a sentence
simile	A **simile** describes a noun using direct comparison with another noun.
colloquialism	A **colloquialism** is a word or phrase used in informal situations.
rhetorical	A **rhetorical** question does not require a response because the answer is already implied.
hyperbole	**Hyperbole** is the use of exaggeration for dramatic effect.
inference	To make an **inference** is to pick up on a meaning not explicitly stated by the author.
synonym	**Synonyms** are two different words with the same, or very similar, meanings.
sibilance	**Sibilance** is the repetition of the 's' sound.
apostrophe	An **apostrophe** can be used in contractions or to show possession.
ellipses	**Ellipses** are used to end speech mid-sentence or to add tension.
technique	A **technique** is a tool used by the writer to produce an effect.
cliché	**Clichés** are techniques that have been overused and have lost their effect.
synthesis	**Synthesis** involves comparing texts and writing about them together.
biased	A non-fiction text is considered **biased** if it presents information in a way that supports a particular point of view.
evidence	An argument should contain **evidence** in order to be considered valid.
convey	You need to be able to explain how writers **convey** their ideas and perspectives.

Now try this

1　Identify the words in the table above that you do not know how to spell correctly.

2　Copy this grid and complete the first column by adding your list of words from question 1. Add any other specific to English Language that you find difficult to spell. Practise each word once a day for a school week, using the **look**, **cover**, **say**, **write**, **check** method.

Word	Monday	Tuesday	Wednesday	Thursday	Friday
simile					

Capital letters

Capital letters are used at the start of a sentence and for proper nouns.

First letter in a sentence

You should start **every sentence** with a capital letter, even if it's within speech marks.

start of a sentence

The old man sighed. "My bus is ten minutes late again," he said.

start of a sentence within speech marks

Proper nouns

Proper nouns always start with a capital letter, wherever they are in a sentence.

Proper nouns	Examples
people, including titles	Atticus Finch, King Charles II, President Obama, David Lloyd-George, Dame Tanni Grey-Thompson
places	London, Antarctic Ocean, Japan, Stratford-upon-Avon, River Ganges, Gulf of Mexico
nationalities and languages	Brazilian/Portuguese, Chinese/Mandarin, British/English
titles of books, plays, films, etc.	*Blood Brothers, Metal Gear Solid, The Colour Purple, King Lear, The Wind in the Willows*
organisations	Pearson, World Wildlife Fund, United Nations, Royal Society of Chemistry
days and months	Monday, Wednesday, Saturday, January, August, December
festivals and other special times	Easter, Diwali, Independence Day, St. Patrick's Day, Id-ul-Fitr, Passover, New Year's Eve
religions and gods	Christianity, Islam, Hinduism, Sikhism, Yahweh, God, Allah, Shiva, Krishna
the pronoun I	The pronoun I is always written as a capital letter.

Short words such as **of** and **the** do not need capitals.

When and when not to use a capital
The lords of the feast greeted the arrival of Lady Macbeth.

In this example, **Lady** has a capital letter because it's referring specifically to Lady Macbeth, and the word **Lady** is her title. However, **lords** doesn't have a capital letter because it's referring to lords in general.

Getting it right

Make sure there is a clear difference between upper and lower case letters in your handwriting so that the examiner can tell which words you have capitalised.

Now try this

Rewrite these sentences with capital letters where needed.

(a) joseph smith founded the church of latter-day saints, whose followers are known as mormons.

(b) On the first wednesday after easter, i have my german exam in berlin.

(c) The north atlantic treaty organisation was founded in 1949 in washington, but its headquarters are in belgium.

Sentence endings

There are three main ways of punctuating the end of a sentence: with a **full stop**, a **question mark** or an **exclamation mark**.

Full stop

Usually, you use a **full stop** to end a statement or a command. This is the most common way of marking the ending of a sentence.

A statement can be fact or opinion.

> Cheltenham in Gloucestershire has a population of about 100,000 people.

This is a command, as the verb 'filter' tells someone what to do.

> Filter the solution to remove the unreacted copper oxide.

Question mark

Always use a **question mark** to show that a question is being asked. The table below shows the three ways of writing a question:

Method	Example question
question word	Which model of the atom is being described?
question tag	That's a rhetorical question, isn't it?
inversion	Is it important to exercise regularly?

Getting it right

In your exams, you **shouldn't** add a question mark to a statement to form a question, even though this is common in speech.

Exclamation mark

An **exclamation mark** is used at the end of an exclamation or to give a statement or command more emphasis. Avoid using exclamation marks in formal writing, except where they appear in a quotation, and never use more than one exclamation mark in a row.

These exclamation marks help to indicate the writer's strength of feeling.

> We must not give in to fear! We must fight injustice wherever we see it!

Golden rule

A sentence is not complete unless you use either a full stop, a question mark or an exclamation mark.

Now try this

Rewrite these sentences, adding the correct punctuation mark to the end of each one.

(a) I think Curley is a menacing character, don't you

(b) The narrator says, "But debt is a debt and must be paid"

(c) It was Mark Twain who said, "One should never use exclamation points in writing. It is like laughing at your own jokes"

(d) What an incredibly stupid thing to do

To revise how to use speech marks correctly, see page 34.

Commas for extra information

Commas are used to make the meaning of your writing clear. One common use of commas is to separate extra information from the main part of the sentence.

Commas to separate words or phrases

You can use commas to separate a **phrase** containing extra information from the rest of the sentence.

> A **phrase** is a group of words that does not contain a verb.

extra information (phrase)   main clause

On 1 September 1939, Germany invaded Poland.

Caliban, the offspring of Sycorax and the devil, was Prospero's slave.

The Pope lives in the Vatican, a city state in the middle of Rome.

Commas to separate clauses

As with a phrase, you need to use commas to separate a **subordinate clause** containing extra information from the rest of the sentence. You often start this clause with a conjunction or relative pronoun.

> A **clause** is a group of words that contains a subject and a verb.

conjunction   extra information (subordinate clause)   main clause

When dawn broke on 1 September 1939, Germany invaded Poland.

relative pronoun

Caliban, who was the offspring of Sycorax and the devil, was Prospero's slave.

relative pronoun

The Pope lives in the Vatican, which is a city state in the middle of Rome.

Golden rule

Use a comma to mark out single words, phrases and clauses from the rest of the sentence.

To learn more about conjunctions, go to page 57.
To learn more about pronouns, go to page 39.

Now try this

Rewrite these sentences, inserting a comma (or commas) to punctuate them correctly.

(a) Because commuters go to work early and return late commuter towns can seem deserted during the day.

(b) Odo and his brother whose name was Robert of Mortain took refuge in Pevensey Castle.

(c) With over a billion followers Islam is the world's second largest religion.

Commas in lists

Commas must be used to separate **items in a list**. Putting commas in the wrong place can change the meaning of the sentence.

Lists of nouns

Commas can be used to separate **nouns** in a list.

list of noun phrases

no comma here

I am going to buy a pair of sandals, two beach towels, some sun cream and a thin T-shirt.

Lists of verbs

Commas can also be used to separate lists of **verbs**.

Getting it right

Use **and** or **or** before the final item in a list instead of a comma.

list of verbs   no comma here   list of adjectives

I will either swim, dive, sail or windsurf on holiday. Watersports are fun, exciting and challenging.

no comma here

Lists of adjectives

You can also use commas to separate two adjectives before a noun where the adjectives have **equal weight**.

Comma here because the adjectives 'interesting' and 'insightful' are equally important.

The scientist published an interesting, insightful paper.

No comma here because 'research' is more important to the meaning of 'paper' than 'interesting'.

The scientist published an interesting research paper.

Now try this

Rewrite these sentences, adding commas in the correct places.

(a) Hard engineering methods for managing floods include building embankments flood walls reservoirs and flood barriers.

(b) The feudal hierarchy consisted of the King his tenants-in-chief their under-tenants and the peasants.

(c) Macbeth is a fearless ambitious nobleman. The Three Witches are strange deceitful and untrustworthy. The porter is a comic minor character.

Avoiding comma splicing

It is easy to make mistakes when joining **main clauses**.

> A **main clause** contains a subject and a verb. It expresses a complete idea.

Run-on sentences

Run-on sentences are a common mistake. In a run-on sentence, two main clauses follow one another without the correct punctuation or conjunction. Here is an example:

main clause 1   missing punctuation/conjunction   main clause 2

> There are few species in the taiga a disease of one species impacts the whole ecosystem.

Comma splicing

Another common mistake is to join two main clauses with a comma. This is called **comma splicing**. Here is an example:

main clause 1   incorrect comma   main clause 2

> There are few species in the taiga, a disease of one species impacts the whole ecosystem.

Avoiding these mistakes

 1   Most of the time, you can simply use a full stop to make **two separate sentences**.

> There are few species in the taiga. A disease of one species impacts the whole ecosystem.

Golden rule

Avoid joining main clauses with a comma. If in doubt, use a full stop.

2   Sometimes, you can use a comma followed by a **conjunction**.

> There are few species in the taiga, **so** a disease of one species impacts the whole ecosystem.

3   Where the two main clauses are linked in meaning, you can use a **semi-colon** to separate the clauses.

> There are few species in the taiga; a disease of one species impacts the whole ecosystem.

To revise how to use commas to separate a subclause from the main clause, see page 26.

Now try this

Rewrite these sentences to correct the comma splicing.

(a) They wanted to go for a walk, they put on their walking boots.

(b) "All animals are equal, some animals are more equal than others."

(c) William invaded in the south, Harold was fighting in the north.

> Two of the sentences need a conjunction adding after the comma. One needs a semi-colon instead of a comma.

Avoiding other comma errors

Misuse of commas is common when adding phrases or clauses of extra information to a sentence.

Restrictive phrases

You must not put commas around a **restrictive phrase**.

restrictive phrase

> The man at the front is taller than the man at the back.

A **restrictive phrase** contains information that is essential to the meaning of the sentence.
A **non-restrictive phrase** provides extra, non-essential information.

The sentence would not make sense if the restrictive phrase **at the front** was removed, so a pair of commas **must not** be used.

That and which

The same idea applies when using **that** and **which**.
That is used to introduce a restrictive clause.
Which is used to introduce a non-restrictive clause.

Here, the writer has more than one house, and this particular one has three bedrooms.

restrictive clause

> My house that has three bedrooms is on a busy road.

no commas either side

Here, the writer has one house and it has three bedrooms.

non-restrictive clause

> My house, which has three bedrooms, is on a busy road.

commas either side

Golden rule

Use a comma before **which**. Do not use a comma before **that**.

Getting it right

Sometimes **which** is used where this page says you should use **that**. It is grammatically correct but wouldn't be the other way round. If you follow the golden rule, you'll always get it right.

Now try this

1 Rewrite these sentences, correcting the positions of the commas.

(a) Thomas Hardy wrote about life, in Wessex which is a historical county.

(b) Sigmund Freud an Austrian, neurologist developed a theory, that humans have an unconscious.

2 Rewrite these sentences, writing **that** or **which** in the gap and adding any missing commas if necessary.

(a) Spits are narrow projections of sand or shingle _____ are attached to the land at one end.

(b) Andheri railway station _____ is one of the busiest stations in the world is in a popular suburb of Mumbai.

Colons

A **colon** is used to introduce further information or explanation.

Colons for further information

You can use a colon to introduce further information after a full sentence, such as a list of items. Here is an example:

Colon introduces a list of items.

> The narrator asked her brother to buy the following: flowers, a bottle of wine and some chocolates.

Do not use a capital letter on the first item after the colon unless it's a proper noun.

You can also use a colon to introduce a more detailed list of items that are separated by **semi-colons**:

To revise using semi-colons in a list, see page 31.

Colon introduces a more detailed list of items.

> The narrator asked her brother to buy the following: some fresh flowers from the stall in the farmers' market; an expensive bottle of wine from the chiller; and some handmade Belgian chocolates.

This list could also be written with bullet points using the same punctuation:

Colon introduces a bullet-pointed list.

> You need to buy the following items:
> • some fresh flowers from the stall in the farmers' market;
> • an expensive bottle of wine from the chiller;
> • some handmade Belgian chocolates.

You can drop the **and** in a bullet-pointed list.

Colons for further explanation

You can use a colon to **separate two parts of a sentence**. The second part can be a phrase or a clause that explains or expands on the first part.

Colon separates the first clause from the phrase.

> Miss Havisham always wore the same things: her wedding dress and only one shoe.

Colon separates two main clauses.

> Miss Havisham's bitter misery stems from one source: she was jilted on her wedding day.

To revise using colons to introduce longer quotes, see page 64.

Now try this

Rewrite these sentences, adding a colon and any other punctuation needed in the correct places.

(a) There was only one thing to do join the revolution!

(b) I need you to find these things for me a knife some tape and a plastic bottle.

(c) A flow map has a clear advantage over others it shows direction and volume of movement.

(d) Italian is quite easy to pronounce most words end with a vowel.

Semi-colons

In general terms, you can think of a **semi-colon** as being halfway between a comma and a full stop. It is used to separate items and to link clauses.

Semi-colons to separate items

You can use a semi-colon to separate detailed items in a list, especially if one or more of the items contains commas. Here is an example:

Only use a capital letter after a semi-colon if the word is a proper noun.

In 1075, three of William's own earls revolted against him: Roger de Breteuil, Earl of Hereford, whose earldom had been reduced in size; Roger's brother-in-law, Ralph de Gael, Earl of East Anglia; and Waltheof, who was the last surviving Anglo-Saxon earl.

Semi-colons separate the detailed items.

In a detailed list, use a semi-colon before the final **and** or **or**.

This list could also be written with bullet points using the same punctuation:

In 1075, three of William's own earls revolted against him:
- Roger de Breteuil, Earl of Hereford, whose earldom had been reduced in size;
- Roger's brother-in-law, Ralph de Gael, Earl of East Anglia;
- Waltheof, who was the last surviving Anglo-Saxon earl.

You can drop the **and** in a bullet-pointed list.

Semi-colons to link clauses

You can use a semi-colon to establish a close connection between two main clauses. The semi-colon joins two clauses into one sentence where the second clause is **linked in meaning** and of **equal importance** to the first clause.

Semi-colon separates the first clause from the second.

Young people tend to move from rural areas to urban ones; older people move from the city to rural areas.

This clause is linked in meaning to the first and is equally as important.

Golden rule

Only use a semi-colon to join two clauses if they are linked in meaning and of equal importance. If in doubt, create two separate sentences using a full stop.

To revise combining main clauses, see page 28.

Now try this

Rewrite these sentences, adding a semi-colon and any other punctuation needed.

(a) We need the following items a large table with sturdy legs a map of Manchester England and two cans of paint which should preferably be green.

(b) The author was finally published in 2017 she had worked for years on her novel.

Brackets and dashes

Brackets and dashes can be used to add extra information to a sentence.

Brackets

You can use a pair of brackets to separate extra information from the rest of the sentence. This information can be a phrase or a clause. Brackets can be placed in the middle or at the end of a sentence. The closing punctuation always goes outside the brackets.

extra information in brackets

> Carl Linnaeus (1707–1778) originally proposed classifying organisms into just two kingdoms.

full stop outside the brackets

> There is further information on commas elsewhere (see pages 26–29).

question mark in clause inside the brackets

> Many people thought that the Earth was flat (how strange was that?).

Two dashes

You can use a pair of dashes to add extra information to a sentence. The extra information can be a phrase or a clause that explains or expands on the first part.

extra information in dashes

> The moose – known as an elk in Europe – is a large herbivore that can eat pine needles.

Single dash

A single dash can be used to mark a break between two clauses or a clause and a phrase.

single dash for suspense

> There was only one thing on his mind – revenge.

Golden rule

If the extra information between pairs of brackets or dashes is removed, the sentence must still make sense.

Getting it right

A single dash is less formal than a colon or semi-colon and generally shouldn't be used in your exams. However, you could use it in the narrative or descriptive writing part of your English Language exam.

Now try this

1 Rewrite this sentence, adding a pair of brackets in the correct place.

   Eating a healthier diet lower fat, sugar and salt can be used to treat cardiovascular disease.

2 Rewrite this sentence, adding a pair of dashes in the correct place.

   The economy of the United States the largest in the world in terms of GDP is approximately a quarter of gross world product.

Hyphens

A **hyphen** is a short, straight line used to join words. A hyphen (-) should not be confused with a dash (–), which is longer. To revise the use of dashes, see page 32.

Joining words together

Hyphens usually **join two or more words** together, but they have other functions too.

Common functions of hyphens	Examples
make compound adjectives	kind-hearted, awkward-looking, user-generated, up-to-date, sugar-free, custom-built, carbon-neutral, well-known
make compound nouns	sister-in-law, self-esteem, editor-in-chief, cul-de-sac, break-in, great-grandmother, fifteen-year-old, passer-by, man-of-war
make compound verbs	to baby-sit, to window-shop, to ice-skate, to double-click, to second-guess, to colour-code
compound numbers	one-third, forty-five
avoid confusion	30 odd books (meaning **30 strange books**) 30-odd books (meaning **approximately 30 books**)
prefix ending in vowel + root word starting with vowel	co-operate, re-enter, anti-aircraft, de-ice
with other prefixes (especially before capital letters)	ex-president, post-apocalyptic, pre-1830, mid-August, anti-American, pro-British
show a word break	King William I created a feudal hier-archy with himself at the top.

Exceptions

There are no hyphens in compound adjectives made with **very** or in adverbs ending in **-ly**, e.g. 'a happily married couple'.

Compound nouns

Many compound nouns can be written in two or three different ways. For example, you can write **paper clip**, **paper-clip** or **paperclip**. Choose one of the ways of writing such words and stick to it. Make sure you don't write **paperclip** in one paragraph and **paper-clip** in the next.

Try to break the word in a sensible place to make it easy to read and understand. For example, **hi-erarchy** or **hiera-rchy** would be clumsy.

Now try this

1 Rewrite this sentence, correcting the positions of the hyphens.

   Barack-Obama is now an-ex president and a-former-commander in chief.

2 Rewrite this sentence, adding hyphens in the correct places.

   Their new pet was an extremely enthusiastic, accident prone, three month old puppy.

Speech marks

Speech marks are used to show the exact words that someone says. They are also known as inverted commas or quotation marks.

Direct speech

Direct speech is usually made up of two parts: a reporting clause and the speech itself. The speech and its punctuation appear between speech marks, and always begin with a capital letter.

reporting clause   speech

Miss Maudie tells Jem, "Things are never as bad as they seem."

The reporting clause can come at the beginning, middle or end of the sentence. This affects the punctuation. Here are some examples:

Speech ends with a comma inside the closing speech mark.   Full stop marks the end of the sentence.

"I ought to be chief," said Jack with a simple arrogance.

Full stop placed within closing speech mark.

"You're talking too much," said Jack Merridew. "Shut up, Fatty."

New speech mark and capital letter used for a new spoken sentence.

No capital letter used here as the same sentence of speech is continuing.

"I climbed a rock," said Ralph slowly, "and I think this is an island."

Comma is used here as the same sentence of speech is continuing.

Ralph shouted at him, "Piggy! Have you got any matches?"

Comma introduces the speech.

Indirect speech

Don't confuse direct speech with **indirect speech**.

"Should I take my umbrella?" asked Harrison.

Direct speech uses speech marks.

Harrison asked whether he should take his umbrella.

Indirect speech does not use speech marks.

Now try this

Rewrite these sentences, adding speech marks and any other missing punctuation for direct speech. Do not change any of the capital letters.

(a) The general ordered Move the cavalry into position

(b) I write for six hours every day replied the author

(c) Why are you so scared asked the girl with the long hair

(d) We don't have a cat he admitted but we do have three dogs

(e) No surrender shouted the protestor.

Contractions

Contractions are made by joining two words together into one shortened form.

Apostrophe placement

When you join two words together to form a contraction, you must add an **apostrophe** where letters have been omitted. Here is an example:

Apostrophe shows where the letter 'a' has been omitted.

you are → you're

Sometimes more than one letter is omitted, and not always from the same place. However, you only ever use one apostrophe:

would have → would've

Apostrophe shows where the letters 'ha' have been omitted.

Apostrophe shows where the letter 'o' has been omitted.

shall not → shan't

The letters 'll' have also been ommitted.

Common contractions

Here are some examples of common contractions with which people often make mistakes. Notice that **I'd** can mean **I would** or **I had**.

Getting it right

Although contractions are acceptable in Standard English, you should avoid them in your exams. However, don't be afraid to use them if you're writing direct speech, as it will make the spoken words sound more natural.

In this contraction, the 'i' changes to an 'o'.

Two words	→	Contraction	Two words	→	Contraction
you are	→	you're	I would	→	I'd
it is	→	it's	I had	→	I'd
we are	→	we're	he has	→	he's
they are	→	they're	they will	→	they'll
who is	→	who's	I shall not	→	I shan't
I will not	→	I won't	we would have	→	we would've
you cannot	→	you can't	you must not	→	you mustn't

Now try this

1 Correct the position of the apostrophe in each of these: did'nt; shouldv'e; wel'l; is'nt; we'rent.

2 Write down the contracted forms of these words: I am; she could have; you might not; who will; that had.

3 Write down each of these contraction as two words: they won't; what're; we've; how's; you can't.

35

Possession: singular

An **apostrophe** can be used to show that an object belongs to someone or something else. It is always attached to the owner, not the object.

Singular nouns

Singular refers to one. Plural refers to more than one. For example, **one dog** is a singular noun, whereas **two dogs** is a plural noun. When you want to show possession by a single owner, simply add an apostrophe and an -s.

owner

There is one priest, so add -'s.

the cassock belonging to the priest → the priest's cassock

the object

More than one theory, but only one Charles Darwin.

Here are some more examples:

Object and owner	→	Apostrophe + -s
the theories of Charles Darwin	→	Charles Darwin's theories
the influence of the novel	→	the novel's influence
the details of the map	→	the map's details

Singular nouns ending in 's'

Some singular nouns end in 's', including people's names. You should treat these in exactly the same way.

object

There is one bus, so add -'s.

the wheels belonging to the **bus** → the bus's wheels

Avoiding apostrophes

If you are not sure where to put an apostrophe, you can reword a sentence to avoid needing one. That way you are less likely to make a mistake.

For example, you might change **Lady Macbeth's** guilt to **the guilt felt by Lady Macbeth**.

Now try this

1 In each phrase, identify the word with the apostrophe in the correct place.

(a) a *monk's* / *monks'* vows

(b) *Angus'* / *Angus's* personality

(c) a *biomes'* / *biome's* climate

(d) Nikita *Khrushchev's* / *Khrushchevs'* leadership

2 Rewrite these phrases, using an apostrophe to show possession.

(a) the results of the investigation

(b) the tone of the article

(c) the doctrines of Islam

(d) the possessions belonging to the deceased man

(e) the geology of the coast

Possession: plural

An **apostrophe** can also be used to show when something belongs to more than one person or thing (a plural noun).

Plurals ending in 's'

The majority of plural nouns end in 's'. When you want to show possession by a plural owner, simply add an apostrophe after the 's'. Here is an example:

There is more than one soldier, so keep the 's' and add an apostrophe.

object   owner

the plan of the soldiers → the soldiers' plan

Here are some more examples:

Object **and owners**	→	's' + apostrophe
the castles belonging to the Normans	→	the Normans' castles
the ideas of the scientists	→	the scientists' ideas
the growth of the megacities	→	the megacities' growth
the themes of the plays	→	the plays' themes

Irregular plurals

Some plural nouns don't end in 's'. Such words work like singular nouns when showing possession, so you add -'**s**. These irregular plurals include the following:

children   women   phenomena   criteria   bacteria   media   stimuli

object   owner   This is an irregular plural noun, so add -'s.

the **rights** of the **children** → the **children's rights**

Golden rule

To show possession by a plural owner:
- when the plural noun ends in 's', add an apostrophe after the 's'
- when the plural noun doesn't end in 's', add -'**s**

Now try this

1 Make the underlined nouns in these phrases plural and move the apostrophe where required:
   the dog's bones; the child's toys; a woman's scarf; the character's motivation; the bacterium's influence.
2 Rewrite this sentence, inserting two apostrophes in the correct places.
   The armies defeat was blamed on the mens lack of experience.

Articles

An **article** is a word you put at the start of a noun phrase to make it either specific or general. An article is a type of **determiner**.

Definite and indefinite articles

The **definite article** is the word **the** and it is used to refer to something specific.

The **indefinite articles** are **a** and **an**. They are used when referring to something in general.

indefinite articles

The river flows through **a** valley and over **an** aqueduct on its way to **the** sea.

definite articles

Golden rule

Use **a** before a word that starts with a **consonant**, or before words starting with 'u' and 'eu' if these make the sound **you**. Use **an** when the following word starts with a **vowel** ('a', 'e', 'i', 'o', 'u') or with a **silent** 'h'.

Whether you use **a** or **an** depends on the first letter of the word that follows the indefinite article. Here are some examples:

a biome   a revolt   a liturgy   a eulogy   a university

Word starts with a consonant.   These letters make the sound **you**.

an abbreviation   an electromagnet   an ultimatum   an hour   an honour

Word starts with a vowel.   Words start with a silent 'h'.

Common mistakes: them/those

There are many other determiners, such as **this, some** and **my**. In non-Standard English, people sometimes use the pronoun **them** instead of the determiner **those**. This is acceptable in informal contexts, but you should never do this in an exam.

Standard English use of **those** rather than non-Standard **them**.

Those cells created by mitosis are called daughter cells.

Common mistakes: a lot

Avoid writing **a lot** as one word. **A lot** is always written as two words, in the same way as **a few**, **a couple** or **a group**. The determiner **a** is not part of the word that follows it.

The scientist experienced **a lot** of problems.

Now try this

Correct the determiners in these sentences.

  (a) A effective way to book an hotel is to use one of them price comparison sites.

  (b) It was a honour to receive such alot of fan mail from an European country.

Different types of pronoun

There are three different types of **pronouns**: personal pronouns, possessive pronouns and relative pronouns. You don't need to remember the names of the different types, but make sure you know how to use them correctly.

Personal pronouns

Personal pronouns replace the name of a person or thing. You use them to avoid repeating the same noun or noun phrase.

> **Stigland** was bishop for more than one area. **He** was accused of simony.

noun

replaces Stigland

Personal pronouns change depending on whether they refer to the **subject** (who is doing the action) or the **object** (who the action is being done to).

plural personal pronouns: **them** (the object), **they** (the subject)

> **I** warned **them**. **They** warned **me**.

singular personal pronouns: **I** (the subject), **me** (the object)

The other personal pronouns are (subject/object) he/him, she/her, it/it, you/you, we/us.

Possessive pronouns

Possessive pronouns show who or what owns something. You can use them with nouns or to replace nouns.

used with a noun

replaces the noun phrase **my work**

> She had copied **my** coursework. It was not **her** work! It was **mine**!

With a noun	my	your	his/her/its	our	their
Instead of a noun	mine	yours	his/hers/its	ours	theirs

Relative pronouns (who, whose, that, which)

Relative pronouns refer back to a noun already mentioned. You can use a relative pronoun to introduce a clause of **extra information** about that same noun. To revise clauses of extra information, see page 26.

refers back to **hydrogen**

> Hydrogen, <u>**which** is an explosive gas</u>, is the lightest element.

extra information (relative clause)

Now try this

1 Rewrite this paragraph, replacing the repeated nouns with the correct pronouns.

Lead is a dense, soft metal. Lead is non-corroding but toxic. Lead's atomic number is 82. The Romans used lead for making Romans' water pipes and lining Romans' baths.

2 Identify the relative pronoun and the relative clause in this sentence.

In 2013, Pope Benedict XVI, whose real name was Joseph Ratzinger, was the first pope to resign since 1415.

Using pronouns

Using **pronouns** correctly will help to make your writing clear and grammatically correct. There are a number of common mistakes you should avoid.

Too many pronouns

It is easy to **overuse** pronouns. It should be clear who you are referring to with every pronoun you use. If in doubt, replace the pronoun with a noun or reword the sentence.

Does the knight go to his own castle or his friend's castle?

> The knight sent a message to **his** friend before **he** went to **his** castle.

Its and it's

These two short words are often confused. **Its** with no apostrophe is a possessive pronoun. **It's** with an apostrophe is a contraction of two words: **it** and **is**.

This contraction means **it is**.

> Mercury is a toxic metal. **It's** a liquid at room temperature because **its** melting point is −39°C.

This pronoun means **the melting point belonging to it** (the mercury).

Me, myself and I

The pronoun **I** refers to the **subject** of a sentence and **me** refers to the **object**.

Ricky and I is the subject.　　　Use **I** as it forms part of the subject.　　　**I** always comes after the other name, not before.

> **Ricky** and **I** revised all day with the girls.

It is a common mistake to use **me** instead of **I** when there is more than one person as the subject. Check which to use by removing the first part of the subject (**Ricky and**) to see whether the sentence makes sense. The above sentence must start with **I**, not **me**.

The same rule can be applied to the **object**. Take **Ricky and** out of the sentence below and see whether the sentence makes sense. Here, **me** must be used rather than **I**.

the object　　　Use **me** as it forms part of the object.

> The girls revised all day with **Ricky** and **me**.

Myself and other **reflexive pronouns** should only be used to refer back to the subject of a sentence.

Reflexive pronoun **myself** refers back to the subject **I**.

You is the correct pronoun for the object of the sentence, not **yourself**.

> I wash **myself** every morning.

> Can I get anything for **you**?

Now try this

Choose the correct pronoun to complete these sentences.

(a) Please would you email it to *I / me / myself*?

(b) Suzie and *I / me / myself* made a discovery.

(c) The examiner was very rude to my brother and *I / me / myself*.

(d) I gave *I / me / myself* a pat on the back.

Less or fewer? Who or whom?

Mixing up **less** with **fewer** and **who** with **whom** are common mistakes that you should avoid in your writing.

Less or fewer?

In non-Standard English, people often use **less** instead of **fewer** before a noun. You should use **fewer** before plural nouns and **less** before singular nouns.

Plural nouns with fewer	fewer regulations	fewer students	fewer tools	fewer beliefs
Singular nouns with less	less sugar	less water	less incentive	one less apple

You should also use **less** with **money, time** and **measurements**. Even though you can count these and they seem to be plural, grammatically they are considered to be **singular** amounts.

Use **less** not **fewer**.   Treat money, time and measurement as a singular amount.

less than £100   less than **two hours**   less than six **feet**

Make sure you use **than** not **then** to make the comparative phrase.

Who or whom?

Who and **whom** are relative pronouns. They refer back to a person already mentioned. If the person being referred to is the **subject** of the action, use **who**. If the person being referred to is the object of the action, use **whom**. To revise relative pronouns, see page 39.

Use **who** because the subject (**a doctor**) is **doing** the action (**specialising**).

A doctor **who** specialises in the treatment of diseases of the nervous system is a neurologist.

Use **whom** because the object (**people**) is **doing** the action to the neurologist (**visiting**).

A neurologist is a doctor **whom** people visit for treatment of diseases of the nervous system.

Whom should also be used after a preposition, although it is mainly used in formal situations.

Use **whom** after the preposition **to**.

To **whom** should I address my letter of complaint?

Expressions of quantity

Some expressions of quantity always use **whom** not **who**, such as **all of whom, some of whom** and **none of whom**. Here is an example:

Land service was provided by peasants, most of whom **were bound to one lord.**

Now try this

1 Write **less (than)** or **fewer (than)** in front of these nouns: distress; mistakes; woodland; abbots; biodiversity; a century; two million pounds; six deities; 25 miles; bacteria.

2 Insert either **who** or **whom** into these sentences.
   (a) James II, _____ was deposed in the Glorious Revolution, died in 1633.
   (b) With _____ are you going to the cinema?
   (c) The scientist _____ we met yesterday just won a prize.
   (d) The papers blamed the politicians, several of _____ have now resigned.

Whose or who's?
That or which?

In addition to **who** and **whom**, it is common to make mistakes with other relative pronouns.

Whose or who's?

The difference between these two words is simple. **Whose** is a relative pronoun that introduces extra information. It means **belonging to** the thing already mentioned.

relative pronoun

The peasants, **whose** complaints had been ignored, rose up in revolution.

extra information (relative clause)

Who's is a contraction of **who is** or **who has**.

contraction meaning **who is**

This is my friend Zhou, **who's** from China.

contraction meaning **who has**

Who's got the answer to question 5?

- -

That or which?

You can insert more information about a noun into a sentence using the relative pronouns **that** and **which**. If the additional information is essential to the meaning of the sentence, use **that**. If the extra information can be left out, use **which**.

To revise relative pronouns, see page 39.

Environmental groups <u>that are interested in energy policy</u> put pressure on governments.

This information is essential: only environmental groups interested in energy policy put pressure on governments.

Environmental groups, <u>which are interested in energy policy</u>, put pressure on governments.

This information could be removed without affecting the meaning: it implies that all environmental groups are interested in energy policy.

She handed in her homework <u>that was finished</u>.

This information is essential: it tells you that only some of her homework was finished and it was only that finished homework that she handed in.

She handed in her homework, <u>which was finished</u>.

This information could be removed without affecting the meaning: it implies that all of her homework was finished and she handed it all in.

- -

Now try this

Rewrite these sentences, inserting **who's**, **whose**, **that** or **which** in the gaps.

(a) The politicians _____ policies led to the problems have escaped any blame.

(b) The effects of climate change, _____ are already being felt around the world, may soon become more intense.

(c) Christian practices ____ people observe in their own homes include praying and Bible reading.

(d) The research scientist, _____ made an exciting discovery, does not want to be interviewed.

Golden rule

Use a comma before **which**. Do not use a comma before **that**.

Have or of?
Effect or affect?

Mixing up **have** and **of** after modal verbs is a common mistake that you should avoid. The difference between **effect** and **affect** is also something you should learn before your exams.

Always use could have, not could of

It is very common for people to use the word **of** instead of **have** after verbs such as **could**, **should** or **may**. The words sound similar, especially when spoken quickly. You should also avoid contractions when writing your exam answers. Here are some examples:

incorrect

The infection **could of** spread. ✗

past tense modal verb

The infection **could have** spread. ✓

grammatically correct and appropriate for exam writing

incorrect

The castle **might of** been captured but for the arrival of the cavalry. ✗

past tense modal verb

The castle **might have** been captured but for the arrival of the cavalry. ✓

grammatically correct and appropriate for exam writing

Golden rule

Always use **have** after a modal verb in the past tense, not **of**.

For information about modal verbs, see page 51.

Effect and affect

Effect and **affect** are two more words you can easily mix up because they sound very similar.

noun (an effect)

The orbit of the Moon has an **effect** on the Earth's tides.

verb (to affect)

The orbit of the Moon **affects** the Earth's tides.

Getting it right

Effect and **affect** are words you'll use a lot in your exams. Remember that **effect** is a noun – a naming word – and **affect** is a verb – an action.

Now try this

1 Rewrite these sentences, inserting **effect** or **affect**.

(a) The increasing population is likely to _____ local services.

(b) The increasing population will have a significant _____ on local services.

2 Rewrite these sentences, correcting the mistakes after the modal verbs.

(a) By 2050, the number of Muslims may of equalled the number of Christians around the world.

(b) Napoleon could of won the Battle of Waterloo but he underestimated the enemy.

(c) I should of realised my mistake, then I might of been able to do something about it.

Negatives

Here are some mistakes to avoid when using **negatives** in exam writing.

Avoid double negatives

The most common way to make a negative is to add the word **not** to a verb.

> The experiment **was** a success.
>
> This is a positive verb.

> The experiment **was** **not** a success.
>
> Adding **not** after the verb makes it negative.

You can also make a negative by adding **no** to a **noun**.

> He's a **hero** of mine.
>
> This is a positive verb.

> He's **no hero** of mine.
>
> Adding **no** before the noun makes it negative.

Using **no** and **not** together makes a **double negative**. Double negatives are often used in non-Standard English. They must not be used in exam writing.

> Macbeth could **not** make **any** sense of the witches' prophesies.
>
> Using **no** here would would be incorrect because it would make a double negative.

Some nouns have **negative forms**, which can also be used to make negatives. For example, **nothing** is the negative form of **anything**. Don't use a negative noun with a negative verb.

> The fussy child **wouldn't** try **anything** new to eat.

Using **nothing** here would be incorrect because it would make a double negative.

> The other negative forms are **none, no one, nobody, neither, nowhere** and **never**.

Doesn't, don't and ain't

These three negative verbs are often misused. **Don't** is a contraction of **do not**. **Doesn't** is a contraction of **does not**. **Ain't** is non-Standard English so do not use it in your exam writing. Use the negative of **to be** or **to have** instead.

Use **don't** after...	Use **doesn't** after...
plural nouns. The results **don't** make sense.	...singular nouns. The car **doesn't** want to start.
the pronouns **I, you, we** and **they**. You **don't** understand.	the pronouns **he, she** or **it**. She **doesn't** listen to my advice.

Getting it right

If you are unsure, read the contraction out in its long form to see if it sounds right.
For example, **"He don't understand!" Anne shouted.** sounds wrong because **do not** is not used with **he**.

Adding **not** after the verb makes it negative.

> The author **is** **not** very good at using similes.

Now try this

Correct the negatives in this paragraph.

Chapter 4 shows that the character don't really have no close friends. He ain't very good in social situations. He don't know nobody in his class. He thinks it ain't fair that he ain't got no one to rely on.

Active and passive

You can write a clause in either the **active** or the **passive** voice.

Active voice

When a clause is in the **active voice**, the subject of the verb is **doing** the action described.

subject   active verb

The clergyman is praying.

The subject is **doing** the verb → **active voice**.

subject   active verb   object

Wellington defeated Napoleon at the Battle of Waterloo.

The subject is **doing** the verb to the object → **active voice**.

Passive voice

When a clause is in the **passive voice**, the action is **done to** the subject.

subject   passive verb

The country's natural resources were exploited.

The action is **done** to the subject → **passive voice**.

Using the active and passive

Both the **active** and **passive** are Standard English. You will use the active voice in most of your writing. In general, use the passive when the person or thing causing the action is not known, or to focus attention on the person or thing being affected.

agent   active verb   subject

Today, economists **released** a very encouraging report.

subject   passive verb   agent

Today, a very encouraging report **was released** by economists.

Getting it right

Read a passive sentence back to yourself. If it sounds clumsy, rewrite it in the active voice.

Now try this

1 Are these clauses active or passive?
   (a) The Jews were persecuted
   (b) His sister had been raised in an orphanage
   (c) The ecosystem had recovered from the pollution
   (d) An adverb can be used to modify a verb
   (e) The soldier fought by himself against the enemy forces

2 Rewrite this clumsy passive sentence in the active voice.

   The lamp was knocked over by Shilpa.

Simple present tense

You use the **simple present tense** to talk about something that is happening in the present, something that is currently or always the case, or something that happens regularly.

The simple present tense can also be used to talk about events in the future (see page 50).

Regular verbs

It is usually easy to form the simple present as most verbs don't change, except when using **he**, **she** or **it**. Here is an example:

> The verb form doesn't change when used with **I**, **you**, **we** or **they**.

to <u>work</u> → **I work; you work; we work; they work**
to <u>work</u> → **he works; she works; it works**

> The verb form changes when used with **he**, **she** or **it**.

Irregular verbs

Some verbs don't follow this pattern in the simple present. These are **irregular** verbs. Notice how, again, the changes only apply to the **he**, **she** and **it** forms.

> When a verb ends in a vowel other than 'e', add -**es**.

> When a verb ends in -**ch**, -**sh**, -**x**, -**s** or -**z**, add -**es**.

Subject	to have	to be	to go	to catch	to hurry
I	have	am	go	catch	hurry
you	have	are	go	catch	hurry
he/she/it	has	is	go<u>es</u>	catch<u>es</u>	hurr<u>ies</u>
we	have	are	go	catch	hurry
they	have	are	go	catch	hurry

> When a verb ends in a consonant plus -**y**, change the 'y' to an 'i' and add -**es**.

Now try this

1. Identify the correct simple present tense spelling in each underlined pair.
   (a) he *lie* / *lies*   **(b)** she *goes* / *gos*   **(c)** he *washes* / *washs*   **(d)** she *burys* / *buries*   **(e)** it *fix* / *fixes*

2. Rewrite these verbs in the simple present tense: I was; you ran; he went; she did; it mixed; he played; she bullied; it fizzed; we stood; they swam.

Present continuous tense

The **present continuous tense** – also called the present progressive – is used to talk about events that are still in **progress** at the time of writing. It is usually formed by using the present tense of the verb **to be** and adding -ing to the main verb.

Example of a verb in the present continuous

Simple present	Present continuous (to be plus -ing)
I learn	I **am** learn**ing**
you learn	you **are** learn**ing**
he/she/it learns	he/she/it **is** learn**ing**
we learn	we **are** learn**ing**
they learn	they **are** learn**ing**

Past continuous tense

The **past continuous** – also called the past progressive – can be formed in a similar way. The only difference is that you use the **past** tense of **to be**: I was **learning**.

Adding -ing

Most verbs follow the rules set out in the table above. However, there are some exceptions where you have to **drop**, **keep** or **add** letters before adding -ing.

1 Verb ends with a silent 'e'.
Rule: Drop the 'e' and add -ing.
hope → I am hoping

2 Verb ends with two vowels.
Rule: Keep both vowels and add -ing.
agree → we are agreeing

3 Verb ends with a 'c'.
Rule: Add 'k' and add -ing.
panic → she is panicking

4 Verb ends with a vowel plus 'l'.
Rule: Double the 'l' and add -ing.
travel → I am travelling

5 Verb has a short vowel sound and ends with one consonant.
Rule: Double the consonant and add -ing.
put → you are putting

6 Verb ends in 'ie'.
Rule: Drop the 'ie' and add -ing.
die → insects are dying

Stressed and unstressed syllables

There are many verbs that end with a **vowel** and a **consonant** that have more than one syllable (e.g. **to target**). Whether or not you double the final consonant when adding -ing depends on the syllable that is stressed. The same rules apply as for adding -**ed** to these verbs.

To find out about these rules, see page 48.

Now try this

Add -**ing** correctly to these verbs: sleep; marvel; have; cancel; plan; enter; enjoy; die; frolic; live; infer.

Simple past tense

You can use the **simple past tense** to talk about an event that has already happened. To form the simple past, you usually add the suffix **-ed** to the verb and change the spelling of the root word.

> **Simple past** and **perfect tense** are different ways of talking about the past:
> • he worked (simple past)
> • he has/had worked (perfect tense).

Single-syllable verbs

Here are some general spelling rules to follow when adding **-ed** to verbs with one syllable:

 Verb ends with **two or more consonants**.
Rule: Add -ed.
to post → posted

 Verb has a short vowel sound and ends with **one consonant**.
Rule: Double the consonant and add **-ed**.
to hop → hopped

 Verb ends with an 'e'.
Rule: Add -d.
to chase → chased

 Verb ends with a consonant and a 'y'.
Rule: Change the 'y' to an 'i' and add **-ed**.
to copy → copied

⑤ Verb ends in a vowel and a 'y'.
Rule: Do not change the 'y' to an 'i'. **Simply** add **-ed**.
to stay → stayed

Multi-syllable verbs ending Vowel–Consonant

The key to adding **-ed** correctly to these types of verbs is to work out if the final syllable is stressed or not. These rules also apply when adding **-ing** to form the present continuous tense.

To revise the present continuous tense, go to page 47.

 The final syllable is **stressed** (e.g. re<u>fer</u> not <u>re</u>fer).
Rule: Double the consonant and add **-ed**.
to re<u>fer</u> → referred

 The final syllable is **not** stressed (e.g. <u>lis</u>ten not lis<u>ten</u>).
Rule: Add -ed.
to <u>lis</u>ten → listened

 Verbs that end with a vowel plus 'l' are an exception to this rule, no matter which syllable is stressed.
Rule: Double the 'l' and add **-ed**.
to distil → distilled

Getting it right

It can be difficult to learn all of the spelling rules that you need to know, so plenty of practice is the best way to make sure you get words like this right in your exams.

Now try this

Add **-ed** correctly to these verbs: host; equal; cancel; outline; study; admit; visit; tidy; stop; follow.

Irregular past tense

Some verbs are irregular in their past tense forms. You must learn how they form the past tense.

Regular verbs

Verbs that are regular in the past tense follow this pattern:

Verb	Simple past tense	Past participle (perfect tense)	Examples
to work	worked	worked	They **worked** very hard. They have **worked** very hard.

Irregular verbs

The following verbs do not follow the pattern above. Make sure you know all of them.

Verb	Simple past tense	Past participle (perfect tense)	Examples
to be	was/were	been	We were late and she was unhappy. She has **been** unhappy.
to go	went	gone	He went home. He has **gone** home.
to take	took	taken	I **took** the bus to town. I have **taken** the bus to town.
to see	saw	seen	I saw you recently. I haven't **seen** you recently.
to give	gave	given	He gave his sister a present. He has **given** a present to her.
to show	showed	shown	The evidence showed who was guilty. The evidence has **shown** who was guilty.
to begin	began	begun	My day began with an accident. My day had **begun** with an accident.
to write	wrote	written	She wrote to her MP. She has **written** to her MP.
to speak	spoke	spoken	She spoke to her coach about her training. She has **spoken** to her coach.
to do	did	done	We did all of our chores. We have **done** all of our chores.
to choose	chose	chosen	He chose a new coat. He has **chosen** a new coat.

Now try this

Correct the past tense verbs in this paragraph.

The day of the battle beginned with a bad decision. The general speaked to his advisors and choosed to place his cavalry far in the rear. However, he hadn't thinked about the poor weather: it had beed raining for days. If he had knowed that the horses would struggle in the mud, then the enemy might not have breaked through and stealed victory.

The future

There is no separate future tense, but there are three ways of using the present tense to speak about the future.

 Going to

One way to form the future tense is to use **going to** after the present tense of the verb **to be**. You use this phrase with another verb.

present tense of **to be**

The author **is going to release** a new novel next year.

present tense indicating a future action

 Will

Another way to form the future tense is to use the modal verb **will** before another verb.

modal verb indicating a future action

The government **will pass** a law to ban certain chemicals this autumn.

 Present tense for the future

You can also talk about the future using a **present tense verb**.

simple present tense

The President **arrives** on Thursday for talks.

You can use the **simple present** to talk about something that has already been scheduled.

present continuous tense

I **am competing** in a maths challenge tomorrow.

You can use the **present continuous** to talk about future plans or arrangements.

Using other verbs to talk about the future

You can use some other **modal verbs**, such as **might** and **could**, to talk and write about the future. You can also use other verbs, like **hope to** and **plan to**. However, none of these verbs express the same certainty as using **will**.

Shall is an alternative to **will** but is only used in formal situations.

Time expressions

Using time expressions can help to indicate whether you are writing about the present or the future: **tomorrow, next year, later, next January, after the holidays.**

Now try this

Rewrite these past tense sentences so that they are about the future, using the method indicated in brackets.

(a) The prisoner escaped from prison and made his way home. (will)

(b) My friend left by train in the morning. (simple present)

(c) The particle physicist revealed her discovery to the world. (going to)

(d) My secondary school class had a reunion this year. (present continuous)

Modal verbs

A **modal verb** is a type of auxiliary verb. This means that it comes before another verb and changes that verb's meaning.

Possibility, ability and necessity

Modal verbs help add shades of meaning to a sentence, and are often used to express **possibility**, **ability** or **necessity**. Here are some common modal verbs and their functions:

Possibility	Ability	Necessity
might, may, could, must, will, shall, would	could, can	should, ought to, must, need to

Notice that some modal verbs can have more than one function.

Modal verbs are different from other verbs because...

- they don't change form according to the person, e.g. I **should**, you **should**, he/she/it **should**, we **should**, you **should**, they **should**
- they come before another verb to change its meaning.

Here are some examples:

modal verbs expressing **possibility**

It **could** take ages to repair the roof.   If we had left earlier, we **might** have made it on time.

modal verbs expressing **ability**

He **can** play the piano brilliantly.   She **couldn't** understand why she had got lost.

You can use **negative** versions of modal verbs too.

In speech, people often contract modal verbs when using the negative. For example, I **couldn't do it**. Most contractions of modal verbs are straightforward, but watch out for the following:

I can not	→	I can't or I cannot
I will not	→	I won't
I would	→	I'd
I will	→	I'll

Getting it right

In your exams, you should avoid using contractions, except for effect in direct speech.

You may also come across the following in older literary texts:

I shall not → I shan't   I ought not → I oughtn't   I may not → I mayn't

Now try this

1 Identify the modal verbs in these sentences and label them **possibility**, **ability** or **necessity**.

　(a) The rumours may be true but I couldn't tell you where they came from.

　(b) You ought to go soon or you could miss your train.

2 Complete these sentences with appropriate modal verbs to show possibility, ability or necessity.

　(a) This _____ end badly," she sighed. (certainty)

　(b) Pollution _____ cause acid rain. (ability)

　(c) You _____ wear safety goggles. (strong necessity)

Subject–verb agreement

You must always make sure the **verb** you use agrees with its **subject** (the person or thing **doing** the action).

Singular or plural nouns

Most of the time, making the subject and verb agree is straightforward.

singular noun   singular verb forms

A **curate** **is** a member of the clergy who **assists** a vicar or parish priest.
Curates **are** members of the clergy who **assist** a vicar or parish priest.

plural noun   plural verb forms

More than one subject

When the subject is made up of **two or more nouns** connected by **and**, use the plural verb form. If the nouns are connected by **or**, use the singular.

The man and the woman **are** on holiday.

plural subject (**they**)   plural verb form

A bee or a wasp **is** in the garage.

two singular nouns (**it** or **it**)   singular verb form

Noun phrases

When the subject includes a **phrase** or **clause** before the verb, make sure the verb agrees with the subject and not with a noun or pronoun in that phrase or clause.

singular subject   phrase   singular verb form

One <u>of our jetfighters</u> **is** missing.
The lady <u>who owns the dogs</u> **drinks** too much coffee.

singular subject   clause   singular verb form

Collective nouns

A collective noun, such as a **team**, **company** or **class**, refers to a group of people or things. It is good practice to treat collective nouns as singular. The main exception to this is **police**, which is always treated as plural. If you're not sure, check in a dictionary.

Singular verb form: a family is made up
of several people but it is one unit.

collective noun

My family **is** from Yorkshire.

Pearson **has** published a revision guide for Edexcel Geography.

All, each and every

Use a **plural** verb form after **all**: All of these chemicals **react** with water.

Use a **singular** verb form after **each** and **every**: Each chemical **reacts** differently with water. Every chemical **reacts** differently with water.

Now try this

Rewrite these sentences, adding the correct form of the verb given in brackets. Use the present tense.

(a) The keys to the door and the vault _____ missing. (to be)

(b) My team _____ every day after school. (to practise)

(c) Each of these sentences _____ a gap to fill. (to include)

(d) Some chemicals and biological agents _____ extremely toxic. (to be)

(e) The military police _____ arrested the fugitive soldier. (to have)

Tense consistency

In general you should choose an appropriate tense and stick to it.
The key to success is to be consistent and not to swap between tenses as you write.
If all the action happens in the same time frame (past, present or future), you must stick to the same tense.

Past tense

In subjects such as History, you should describe events using the past tense.

past tense   *present tense*

The king rallied his supporters, suppressed the rebels and punishes the conspirators. ✗

This version is incorrect because the tense changes within the same time frame.

The king rallied his supporters, suppressed the rebels and punished the conspirators. ✓

This version is correct because the tense remains consistent within the same time frame.

Present tense

In English Literature, you use the present tense to describe characters and their actions.
In English Language, you use it to analyse how a writer uses language and structure.

present tense   *past tense*

Pip is passionate, has a strong conscience and wanted to improve himself. ✗

This version is incorrect because the tense changes.

Pip is passionate, has a strong conscience and wants to improve himself. ✓

This version is correct because the tense remains consistent.

present tense   *past tense*

The writer uses a series of short sentences, which created a build-up of tension and highlights how much danger the narrator was in. ✗

present tense   *past tense*

This version is incorrect because the tense alternates between present and past.

The writer uses a series of short sentences, which creates a build-up of tension and highlights how much danger the narrator is in. ✓

This version is correct because the tense remains consistent.

Now try this

1 Rewrite this passage so that the tense is consistently in the present.

Magnesium was a silvery-white metal. It ignited easily in air and burns with a bright light. It is an essential element to life but it did not occur uncombined in nature.

2 Rewrite this passage so that the tense is consistently in the past.

In 1204, an army of about 20,000 soldiers breaks into the city of Constantinople. This army of the Fourth Crusade looted, pillages and is going to slaughter its way through the great city.

Paragraphs

A **paragraph** is a group of sentences. Usually, sentences are grouped together because they are about the same thing. Using paragraphs presents your writing in an organised, logical way.

TiPToP

It can be tricky to know when to start and when to end a paragraph. As a general rule, you should start a new paragraph when something changes. You can use **TiPToP** to help you remember to start a new paragraph when the **Time, Person, Topic** or **Place** changes.

Change of time

These sentences are about the 1920s.

... Between 1921 and 1924, there was a period of hyperinflation in the Weimar Republic in Germany, which caused significant internal political instability.

     Today, the German economy is much more stable with inflation at around 2%...

Leave an indent to mark the start of a paragraph.   These sentences are about the present day.

Change of person (including who is speaking)

These sentences are about what Milly thinks and says.

... Milly was not convinced by Shanice's pleas. She had heard it all before. "You always say you're going to pay me back, Sha. But you never do. You still owe me twenty quid," Milly complained.

     "What? Twenty? It was ten, wasn't it?" replied Shanice. "I'm good for it tomorrow. Trust me, babel!"

New paragraph for a change of person and speaker.   These sentences are about what Shanice says.

Change of topic

These sentences present one point of view.

... Many people argue that large-scale deforestation leads to environmental problems. For example, top soil is exposed and eroded, leaving the land more at risk of flooding.

     However, farmers in developing countries argue that large-scale clearances free up valuable land for the cultivation of crops for export, such as soya ...

Start the new paragraph with a conjunction.   These sentences present a different point of view.

Change of place

These sentences are about the revolt in one place.

... During the revolt, Roger, the Earl of Hereford, was blocked from taking his troops across the River Severn by Bishop Wulfstan and the abbot of Evesham.

     Over in the east, the Anglo-Saxons joined the Normans to prevent Ralph de Gael's troops breaking out of East Anglia ...

Start the new paragraph with the new location.   These sentences are about the revolt in a different place.

Marking up corrections

When you check and correct your writing, insert a **double slash** (//) to mark where you will start a new paragraph in a revised version of your work.

Now try this

What does TiPToP stand for? What does it remind you to do?

Introductions

An **introduction** needs to engage the reader and set the tone for your writing. Before you start your introduction, make sure you are clear about your purpose and audience.

Writing to present a viewpoint

A good way to start a piece of **writing to present a viewpoint** is to grab your reader's attention in the very first sentence. Don't tell your reader what you are going to write about. Get straight to the point by using one of the following ideas.

Start with...	Examples
a statement.	Organised mass religion will eventually become irrelevant to human lives. Make it bold or controversial for extra impact.
a question.	Have you ever wondered what it would be like to live without access to clean drinking water? A rhetorical question invites the reader to think about their own experiences.
a quotation.	"Life's but a walking shadow, a poor player That struts and frets his hour upon the stage" (Macbeth, Act 5, Scene 5) The quotation must be relevant to the theme of your answer.
a fact or statistic.	There are more than 10,000 distinct religious groups in the world. Surprising or shocking facts will make a bigger impression.
an anecdote.	For the first nine years of my life, I was raised on a farm and developed a good understanding of animal welfare. Make sure your anecdote is short, relevant and interesting.

Imaginative writing

When you start a piece of **imaginative writing**, try to make your reader feel as if they have been thrown into the scene. Use these ideas to make the reader want to know more.

Start with...	Examples
a vivid description.	The market was a riot of colour and noise. Rickety tables groaned under the great platters of pungent-smelling spices. Use a mix of senses to evoke the setting.
interesting dialogue.	"I told you not to do that," growled Ali. "But, you, you said ..." spluttered Ahmed in disbelief. Ali laughed mirthlessly. "Too late, mate. I'm going to have to tell." Use interesting verbs and adverbs to make your reader infer what the characters might be talking about.
a sense of mystery, conflict or danger.	It was almost completely dark inside and silent as a grave. As the door closed behind me, the darkness and silence seemed almost solid. Leave the reader guessing.

Now try this

Write the opening paragraph for each of these tasks.

(a) Mobile phones only affect society in a negative way. Write a speech explaining your point of view on this statement.

(b) Write an imaginative description of a time when you or someone you know received some surprising news.

Conclusions

A strong **conclusion** leaves the reader with a lasting impression. Make sure you plan how you are going to finish your piece of writing to present a viewpoint or imaginative writing before you start.

Writing to present a viewpoint

A good conclusion in a piece of writing to present a viewpoint will neatly summarise your points into a central idea. Avoid repeating any ideas in detail at this stage. For extra impact, try using the following ideas for your final sentences.

Idea	Examples
End with an image.	The churches are all closed now. They are empty, crumbling and stripped bare of precious metals that have been recycled to power our new glowing objects of worship: the screens on our phones. Use vivid vocabulary to make your reader imagine the scene.
End with a question.	How long will it be until you too are replaced by a robot? A rhetorical question leaves the reader with something to think about.
End with a warning.	We may still have time to repair the damage. If we don't act now, future generations will look back in despair. Your warning must refer back to actions you have suggested previously in the text.
End with a call to action.	Do not turn away and hope someone else will deal with it. Help make a difference by joining a litter patrol today. Use the imperative form of the verb to make it clear what the reader should do next.
End on an uplifting note.	One person can make a ripple, but a community can make waves that clean up the locality and change things for the better. Make sure your point emphasises positive outcomes.

Imaginative writing

Pieces of **imaginative writing** also need a strong ending. Here are some ideas to follow and certain things to avoid in order to achieve this.

✓ Plan the **tone** of your ending in advance.	✗ Do not **change mood**. If your piece of writing has been serious and tense, avoid making the ending light-hearted and jokey.
✓ Your **final sentence** must have impact, as it is the last thing the examiner will read.	✗ Do not use **clichéd endings** or sudden twists.
✓ Make sure your writing reaches a **resolution** where conflicts are resolved and all loose ends are tied up.	✗ Avoid an anti-climax by making the ending **too long**. Keep your ending just long enough for a satisfactory resolution.

Now try this

Write an imaginative final paragraph for this task.

Describe a time that you or someone you know finished a difficult task.

Conjunctions

Use **conjunctions** to link words, phrases or clauses together. Conjunctions act like signposts so you can also use them very effectively to help structure and order your writing.

Using conjunctions in your writing

There are many different conjunctions you can use in your writing. Here are some examples:

Useful conjunctions for...	Examples
adding and explaining a point:	
first, second, third... in addition... furthermore... moreover... likewise... similarly... subsequently... as a result... therefore... so... consequently... accordingly... hence... thus... lastly...	• One month's rain fell overnight. Consequently, the river swelled and burst its banks. • Lastly, the evidence from the clinical trials is conclusive. The authorities will therefore grant the new drug its licence.
illustrating and emphasising a point:	
indeed... for example... for instance... in particular... especially... certainly... evidently... undoubtedly... to illustrate... significantly...	• Evidently, Napoleon's invasion of Russia was a disaster. • Children in particular are vulnerable to diseases caused by contaminated water.
comparing and contrasting:	
but... however... by contrast... yet... although... conversely... notwithstanding... nevertheless... nonetheless... despite... instead... whereas...	• Although 44% of people in the UK define themselves as Christian, nearly half of the population identifies as having no religion. • Her first novel was a commercial failure, but it was ground-breaking nonetheless.
showing time:	
then... next... before... at that time... after... later... meanwhile... previously... at the same time... while... when...	• Meanwhile, the conditions for workers in the slums were deteriorating. • When Orwell wrote *Animal Farm*, he wanted to counter the positive image of Stalin held by some leaders in the British Government.
summarising and making judgements:	
to conclude... in conclusion... in short... to summarise... in summary...	• To conclude, the main theme of the poem is the enjoyment of raw nature.

For examples of useful longer phrases that you can use in a similar way, see page 58.

Now try this

1 Rewrite this passage, adding these conjunctions in the appropriate gaps: as a result; although; however; for example; when; subsequently.

In 1893, New Zealand was the first country to grant voting rights to women. _____, other countries followed, _____ many only granted limited rights. _____ World War I began, women took on roles and jobs traditionally done by men. _____, they worked as railway guards, firefighters and bank clerks. _____, the suffrage movement gained further momentum. _____, it took until 1928 for women to be granted full voting rights in Britain.

2 Try using some of the conjunctions from the table above in your next pieces of extended writing.

Useful essay phrases

Essay phrases give your writing structure and help you to explain your points more effectively.

Useful phrases for...	Examples
adding and explaining a point:	
it seems that... this suggests that... this creates the impression that... this creates the effect of... it has been established that... it could be argued that... this could be interpreted as... another key point to remember is... in order to understand... of central concern is...	• The rhythm of the poem creates the impression of a steam train travelling at speed through the night. • In order to understand why Miss Havisham manipulates Pip, we must realise that she is driven by a grotesque desire for revenge.
explaining further:	
to put it another way... that is to say... to that end... with this in mind... as a consequence... as a result of this...	• Green plants are essential. That is to say, there would be no other life on Earth without them.
illustrating and emphasising a point:	
this means/makes it clear that... this is proven/evidenced/illustrated by... this view is supported by... to say nothing of... not only... but also... as we have seen... in light of the evidence... by the same token...	• This view is supported by the archaeological evidence from the battlefield. • Not only is China the world's most populous country, but it also has the world's largest standing army.
comparing and contrasting:	
on the other hand... on the contrary... having said that... that being said... despite this...	• The chroniclers of the time suggest that the king was wise and fair. Despite this, he suffered from a poor reputation over the centuries that followed.
summarising and making judgements:	
all things considered... above all... the most/least persuasive argument seems to be... the most significant event was... the dominant theme is... the prevailing attitude was...	• Above all, it is the author's use of imagery that captures the reader's attention. • The prevailing attitude of the time was anti-Semitic and xenophobic.

Essay phrases can be used to improve your extended exam answers. Try to include some of the ones listed on this page in your writing.

Now try this

Rewrite this passage, adding these useful phrases in the appropriate gaps: this means that; that is to say; for these reasons; not only... but also; in order to understand.

_____ the importance of the Qur'an in Islam, you must recognise that Muslims believe it is a sacred 'received' text. _____, they _____ believe the words were revealed to the Prophet Mohammed directly by Allah _____ believe those words have not been altered since. _____ Islamic people view the Qur'an as the ultimate source of guidance and treat it with reverence. _____, Muslims do not speak, eat or drink when someone is reading the Qur'an.

Comparisons

You can use a **comparative** or a **superlative** adjective to compare one thing to another or to a group.

Comparatives

You use a **comparative** to compare two things. The way you write it depends on the number of syllables in the adjective. In general, you add the suffix **-er** to a single-syllable adjective.

> The population of India is larger than the population of Bangladesh.

comparative adjective (large + -er = larger) followed by **than**

If the adjective has two or more syllables, you usually use **more** or **less** before the adjective.

> Macbeth is more ambitious than his friend Banquo.
> Banquo is less ambitious than his friend Macbeth.
> Lady Macbeth is as ambitious as her husband.

The adjective does not change.

Golden rule
Use either **-er** or **more** or **less** to form a comparative. Never combine them.

Irregular comparatives and superlatives
Some comparative and superlative adjectives are **irregular**. Make sure you learn them:
good/better/best
bad/worse/worst
many/more/most
little/less/least
far/farther/farthest

Superlatives

You use a **superlative** to compare a person or thing with everyone or everything else in a group. In general, you add the suffix **-est** to a single-syllable adjective.

> Currently, the Burj Kalifa is the tallest building in the world.

superlative adjective (tall + -est = tallest)

If the adjective has two or more syllables, you usually use **most** or **least** before the adjective.

The adjective does not change.

> Lady Macbeth is perhaps the most interesting of all the characters.
> Some people think *The Tempest* is Shakespeare's least accessible play.

Golden rule
Use either **-est** or **most** or **least** to form a superlative. Never combine them.

Now try this

1 Write the comparative form of these adjectives (**more**, **-er**): old; large; thin; peaceful; easy; unusual; sad; angry; narrow; generous.

2 Now write the superlative form of the same adjectives (**most**, **-est**).

Clauses

There are many different types of **clauses**. Some express a complete idea on their own and can be sentences by themselves because they include a finite verb. Others do not express a complete idea on their own and must be joined with other clauses to make a sentence.

Main clauses

This type of clause contains a **subject** and a **finite verb** and expresses a complete thought. In other words, it makes sense on its own.

A big dog barked.

subject — finite verb

> A finite verb is a verb that has a subject.

A main clause may also contain an **object** and **extra information**.

In the winter of 1069–70, Norman troops burned down people's houses.

extra information (adverbial phrase)   subject   verb   object

Other clauses

A **subordinate clause** contains a subject, verb and object but still does not express a complete idea on its own. To form a sentence, it must be attached to a main clause using a subordinating conjunction such as **when, as, while, because, although, since, until, after** or **where**.

subordinating conjunction

When the dog barked, our cat ran away.

subordinate clause   main clause

A **relative clause** is a type of subordinate clause that adds detail to the subject of the main clause and begins with a **relative pronoun**. It can't be placed at the start of a sentence. There are only four relative pronouns: **who, whose, that** and **which**.

relative pronoun   object

Anne Hathaway, **who was three months pregnant**, married William Shakespeare in 1582.

relative clause   main clause

Minor sentences

Minor sentences are grammatically incomplete because they do not contain a verb. For example, if your teacher asked your age you might reply, **"Fifteen, sir."** Minor sentences are most often used in speech and in short answers. Avoid using them in extended exam answers, apart from for effect in imaginative writing: **There was nothing I could do. Powerless, helpless, directionless.**

Now try this

1   Identify the subject and the verb in each of these main clauses.

  (a) The world population reached 7 billion in 2011.

  (b) Every year, most major cities hold public marathons.

2   Identify the subordinate or relative clause in each of these sentences. State which is which.

  (a) Although it has a cell wall, a bacterial cell is not a type of plant cell.

  (b) Normans believed in making acts of penance, which included building churches or giving gifts to the Church, to make up for the violence.

Simple sentences

A **simple sentence** consists of a single main clause with a finite verb. It can be used effectively in writing to present a viewpoint or imaginative writing.

A subject and one verb

A simple sentence is the most basic sentence type because it contains one clause with one verb. There is also a subject and often an object.

> Crude oil is a complex mix of hydrocarbons.
>   subject   verb   object

Questions and **commands** are also often simple sentences with small changes to word order.

> How serious was the threat of invasion?
>   verb   subject

> (You) Email me as soon as possible.
> (implied) subject   verb   object

Commands have an **implied** subject, which is **you**. Implied means that you don't actually say the subject but you can tell who it is.

Using simple sentences

Simple sentences are usually short, so use them to make clear and important points.
Any elaboration of your point would be better in a **multi-clause sentence**. Here is an example:

> Because the vegetation intercepts precipitation, a rainforest regulates the heavy rainfall of the equatorial climate and reduces the flood risk. It acts like a giant sponge.

A multi-clause sentence explains in detail.   A simple sentence summarises the idea.

For information on multi-clause sentences, see pages 62–63.

In **imaginative** writing, you can use **simple** and **minor sentences** to build up tension. Here is an example:

> Suddenly, it was dark. The night air was motionless. It was the silence that troubled him. It was profound. *Undisturbed. Pure.*

     simple sentences   Minor sentences used for emphasis.

To revise minor sentences, see page 60.

Getting it right

Use simple sentences to make clear, important points. Avoid using too many or your writing will seem too simplistic.

Now try this

Label the subject (S), verb (V) and object (O) in each of these simple sentences.

(a) Waltheof informed Archbishop Lefranc about the revolt.
(b) Clip the slide securely onto the stage.
(c) Mitosis is a type of cell division.
(d) Effective writing uses a variety of sentence types.
(e) Was this the end of Anglo-Saxon resistance?

Compound sentences

You can join clauses together in a number of ways. A **compound sentence** is a type of multi-clause sentence. It contains two or more main clauses linked by a **coordinating** conjunction.

Linked main clauses

The clauses in a compound sentence do not depend on each other for meaning. They express **a complete on their own**, and are linked in different ways by coordinating conjunctions. **And**, **but** and **or** are the most frequently used coordinating conjunctions. Others include **so**, **yet**, **for** and **nor**. Here are some examples:

Tropical cyclones start near the equator and the storms move westwards.

main clause 1   **And** joins similar ideas of equal weight.   main clause 2

Sensory neurones carry impulses to the central nervous system but motor neurones carry impulses from the central nervous system.

But joins contrasting ideas.

Charles I could flee or he could fight.

Or signals alternatives.

To revise the different types of clause, see page 60.

Using compound sentences

You should use compound sentences to link ideas, especially when those ideas are of equal importance. Although each clause could form a sentence on its own, joining them together can connect your ideas more strongly and make your meaning clearer.

These three **simple sentences**...

Interest rates soared. The economy went into recession. It soon recovered.

main clause 1   main clause 2   main clause 3

can be linked to make one compound sentence:

coordinating conjunctions

Interest rates soared and the economy went into recession yet it soon recovered.

main clause 1   main clause 2   main clause 3

Don't join too many clauses together in this way as it soon starts to sound clumsy.

Now try this

Rewrite each pair of these sentences as a compound sentence, by linking them with a suitable coordinating conjunction.

(a) Most scientists agree that the Earth's climate is warming. A few deny it may be caused by human activity.

(b) Siddhartha Gautama was shocked by the suffering he witnessed outside his palace. He left his life of luxury to search for answers.

Complex sentences

Like a compound sentence, a **complex sentence** also has multiple clauses. However, in a complex sentence, one of the clauses is dependent on another clause for meaning.

Subordinate clauses

A **subordinate clause** must be attached to a main clause to express a complete idea. It can come at the beginning, middle or end of a complex sentence and is often linked to another subordinating clause by a subordinating conjunction.

Subordinate clause at the beginning:

subordinating conjunction   subordinate clause

As soon as William took control of Warwick, Edwin and Morcar and their men submitted to William.

main clause   Use a comma after the subordinate clause.

Subordinate clause in the middle:

A church, which is often built in the shape of a cross, is a Christian place of worship.

Use a pair of commas around the subordinate clause.

Subordinate clause at the end: Don't use a comma if the main clause comes first.

Only tough, short grasses survive in the tundra because there is so little heat and rainfall.

Relative clauses

A relative clause is a type of subordinate clause that usually starts with a relative pronoun (**who**, **whose**, **that** or **which**).

To revise subordinate and relative clauses, see page 60.

Using complex sentences

Use complex sentences to express sophisticated ideas, especially when you wish to explain further and add context. They add layers of detail and make your meaning clearer.

These three **simple sentences** can be combined to make one **complex sentence**.

main clause 1   main clause 2   subordinate clause 1   subordinate clause 2

William had always trusted his wife Matilda's leadership skills. Matilda died. William was devastated.

When Matilda died, William, who had always trusted his wife's leadership skills, was devastated.

main clause 3   main clause

This complex sentence gives a clearer indication of why William was devastated.

Now try this

1 Identify the subordinate clause(s) and the main clause in these complex sentences.
   (a) Christian meetings were dangerous because the Romans persecuted them.
   (b) If a population was allowed to grow too much, famine would result, which would reduce the population size.

2 Rewrite each pair of simple sentences as a complex sentence with an appropriate subordinating conjunction or relative pronoun.
   (a) Aluminium oxide is dissolved in molten cryolite. This reduces the temperature needed for electrolysis.
   (b) I heard the news. I dropped my phone in surprise.

Using quotations

You can use **quotations** from a text to provide evidence for your idea or argument. You must use quotation marks (also called speech marks) and other elements correctly to show exactly what you are quoting and why.

Short quotations

You can support your point by including a few well-chosen words from the text in your sentence.

Quoting from prose:

> The report concludes that inequality should be tackled "as an urgent national matter".

Use speech marks around the exact words.

Quoting from a poem:

> In 'Sonnet 130', Shakespeare describes his mistress' eyes as "nothing like the sun", which surprises the reader.

Use single quotation marks for titles.

Quoting from a play:

> In Act 1, Scene 5, Lady Macbeth worries that her husband is "too full o' the milk of human kindness" to seize the crown.

Use speech marks around the exact words, including any unusual punctuation.

- -

Longer quotations

You can use a **colon** to introduce a longer quotation. Make sure you copy the punctuation and layout of the quotation as it appears in the text.

Quoting from prose:

Use the number or name of the chapter for novels.

> Scout shows her innocence when she tells Jem in Chapter 23: "I think there's just one kind of folks. Folks."

Quoting from a poem:

> In 'Envy', the poet tells us to nurture our own unique talents: "With care and culture all may find / Some pretty flower in their own mind".

Use a forward slash to indicate a line break.

Quoting from a play:

Include the act and scene when quoting from plays.

> In Act 1, Scene 3, Julius Caesar is aware of the threat Cassius poses: "Yond Cassius has a lean and hungry look; / He thinks too much, such men are dangerous."

- -

Now try this

Practise writing quotations. Choose one play, one poem and one novel and find an effective quotation in each. Write down a sentence that explains what the quotation tells us, including the quotation itself in speech marks.

Use the examples on this page to help you. Make sure you include references to the name of the poem, chapter name or number in the novel, and act and scene numbers in the play.

Synonyms

Synonyms are words with the same or a very similar meaning.

Why use them?

It is important you use synonyms when writing exam answers as they help you avoid repeating the same words too much, and they can add interest, precision and impact to your writing.

Key words

You should practise using a range of synonyms for **key words** that you use a lot in your writing. From the list of synonyms that you might find in a thesaurus, always try to pick the most precise word for the meaning you are trying to convey. Here are some useful synonyms for essay writing:

Key word	Synonyms
idea	belief, concept, point, opinion, notion, theory, thought, intention, plan
people	consumers, workers, population, general public, community, citizens, inhabitants, populace, person in the street
problem	argument, concern, issue, contention, puzzle, topic, subject, difficulty, drawback, disadvantage
evidence	clue, data, indication, sign, testimony, symptom, declaration, demonstration, proof, support
said	announced, claimed, suggested, disclosed, reported, revealed, implied, remarked, added

Although these words are all synonyms for the noun **problem**, they have different, precise meanings that make them suitable for different contexts. The meanings can be similar (e.g. **topic** and **subject**) or very different (e.g. **puzzle** and **disadvantage**).

Here's an example of how you could use synonyms to vary and improve your writing.

This version is repetitive and uses imprecise language:

repeated words

The scientists said that they now had the evidence to support the idea but said that they had a problem with some of the evidence. ✗

imprecise words

This version is much improved:

Use synonyms to avoid repeated words.

The scientists announced that they now had the evidence to support the theory but disclosed that they had concerns about some of the data. ✓

Use more precise synonyms to convey exact meaning.

Now try this

Rewrite this passage, replacing the underlined words with more precise synonyms.

In some countries, many people now live in megacities. A megacity has at least 10 million <u>people</u>. <u>People</u> are drawn to such cities from urban areas hoping for greater opportunities. This can have a negative effect on the <u>people</u> left behind. Megacities are growing fast. For example, <u>the number of people</u> in Mumbai doubled between 1991 and 2013.

Checking your work

Checking your work is one of the most effective ways to improve your SPaG marks.

Proofreading

Try to check as many questions as you can, especially those where SPaG marks are awarded. If you have time, check your writing three times: once for **spelling**, once for **punctuation** and once for **grammatical sense**. Here are some tips for efficient, speedy proofreading.

Check at the end

Avoid checking each answer as you go. Otherwise you will just see what you **think** you wrote, rather than what you **actually** wrote. Give it some time and pretend you've never seen your answer before or even that it is someone else's writing!

Check for common spelling errors

You won't have time to check every single word, so scan the text for **common errors**, such as **misused homophones**. Pay close attention to words such as **its** and **it's**, **to** and **too**, **effect** and **affect**, and **should of** instead of **should have**. Stop and check that you have used the right one. To revise common spelling errors, see pages 12–15.

Try different spellings

If you spot a word you think you have misspelled, but you are not sure how to spell it correctly, try writing the word **three or four different ways** in the margin and pick the one that looks most correct.

Check the basic punctuation

Scan each sentence for a capital letter at the start and a punctuation mark at the end. Make sure proper nouns have capitals too. Look at the apostrophes you've used; if you can't explain to yourself why you need one, you probably don't. Make sure any direct speech and quotations are within speech marks.

Check it makes sense

Read your answer **'aloud in your head'**. If it sounds clumsy or doesn't make sense, you may have missed out a word or two, or made a common grammatical error, such as switching tenses. To revise switching tenses, see page 53.

Check the organisation

Finally, check that you have divided your answer up logically into paragraphs, so that each paragraph is about the same **time**, **person**, **topic** or **place**. If you have forgotten to start a new paragraph, insert a **//** symbol to show where one paragraph ends and the next one begins. To revise how to construct paragraphs, see page 54.

Now try this

1 Proofread this short passage. Underline all the mistakes you can find.

Having too lords would of been difficult for them barons with lands in both normandy and england. indeed, many of the importantest barons was in this postion. These nobles would of had to deal with to different administrations, two tax systems and two diffrent systems of militry obligations

2 Rewrite the passage correctly.

It is important that you leave yourself some time at the end of the exam to check your work. Correcting a few SPaG mistakes might make the difference you need to improve your grade.

Correcting errors

When you check your work, you may wish to correct something. You can do this by **deleting**, **correcting** or **adding** text.

Deleting text

Draw a **single line** through any words, sentences or paragraphs that you want to remove.

> One of the themes of Shakespeare's *The Merchant of Venice* ~~by William Shakespeare~~ is social injustice.
> — repeated information

Correcting text

To correct a single word or short phrase, draw a line through it and **write the correction above it**. To correct a spelling, cross out and replace the whole word, not just the incorrect letter(s).

>   The Merchant   injustice
> One of the themes of Shakespeare's ~~the merchent~~ of Venice is social ~~media~~.
> — missing capital letters and misspelling   wrong word

Adding text

To add a **single word or short phrase**, put a **caret symbol** (^) below the line to show exactly where the text should go. Then, write the word(s) above the line.

>   missing word
>   themes
> One of the ^ of Shakespeare's *The Merchant of Venice* is social injustice.

To add a **longer piece of text**, use an **asterisk** (*) to mark the exact place you want the new text to go. Write out the new text nearby, either in the margin or underneath the passage.

>   Asterisk shows where text is missing.
> One of the themes of Shakespeare's *The Merchant of Venice* is social injustice.*
> The plot concerns a merchant who is forced to default on a loan.
>
> *The play also deals with the themes of prejudice, love and money.
> — Additional sentence is also marked with an asterisk.

New paragraph

If you have forgotten to start a new paragraph, use the **//** symbol between the two relevant sentences to show where the new paragraph should start.

Now try this

Correct the mistakes in these sentences, using the guidance on this page to help you.

(a) The Domesday Book is a nother exampel of king williams' growing power over conquered kingdom.

(b) Satellites are yoused spot tropical cyclones and to track there progres.

(c) Starting a piece writing can difficult. You need to the readers attention.

Improving answers: History

This extract from a student's answer to a History question contains a number of errors, as well as missed opportunities to score highly for SPaG. The improved response corrects the errors and adds impact by using more accurate and sophisticated SPaG techniques.

These types of improvements can easily be applied to other subjects, so it is worth looking at all the other worked examples on pages 69–75.

Worked example

'There has been huge progress in the prevention of disease since c.1900.'
How far do you agree? Explain your answer.

(16 marks, plus 4 marks for SPaG and use of specialist terminology)

Response with errors

I agree that there has been huge progress in the prevention of diseases since 1900. In the first half of the 20th century, **things** were developed against more and more diseases, such as diphtheria and polio. **Only the most richest** people could afford to get themselves vaccinated. This changed as the **goverment** paid for **kids** to receive the diphtheria vaccine during the **second world war** and thereafter for other vaccines. This means that **loads of people** are now **cured** from such **diseases. This** shows the huge progress made in preventing disease...

Key:
X = error
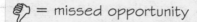 = missed opportunity

X   imprecise vocabulary
X   informal vocabulary
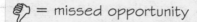   adverbial would help
X   superlative error
X   common spelling error
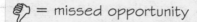   clauses could be joined
X   capitalisation error

Improved sample answer

I agree that there has been huge progress in the prevention of diseases since 1900. In the first half of the 20th century, **vaccines** were developed against more and more diseases, such as diphtheria and polio. **At first,** only the **richest** people could afford to get themselves vaccinated. This changed as the **government** paid for **children** to receive the diphtheria vaccine during the **Second World War** and thereafter for other vaccines. This means that **the vast majority of people** are now **immune** to such **diseases, which** shows the huge progress made in preventing disease...

Key:
✓ = correct use
👍 = improvement

✓   precise vocabulary
✓   formal vocabulary
👍   adverbial orders events
✓   correct superlative adjective
✓   correct spelling
👍   **which** creates complex sentence
✓   capitals for historical period

Now try this

Look back at a piece of writing you have done for History recently.

(a) Check it three times: firstly for spelling mistakes, secondly for punctuation errors and finally for grammatical sense. Aim to find at least five mistakes.

(b) Write out a corrected version. Can you find ways of making your sentence constructions more sophisticated too?

Improving answers: Geography

This extract from a student's answer to a Geography question contains a number of errors, as well as missed opportunities to score highly for SPaG. The improved response corrects the errors and adds impact by using more accurate and sophisticated SPaG techniques.

Worked example

Study the three options for the USA.
Select one option you think would be best for the environment and for the USA. Justify your choice.

(12 marks, plus 4 for SPaG)

Response with errors

I think the pipeline would be the best **option, this** is because a lot of people would get jobs and the US states along the route would get more tax. It would also save the **united states** from having to import so much **oil. I** don't think that the **enviromental** costs are a major **problem, the** Ogallala Aquifer does not appear to be a very important area for wildlife. The amount of carbon dioxide created might add to global warming but so far the changes to the climate have been **small. However,** drilling for oil in the Western **Artic** Reserve is not a good option, because the roads and drilling pads **pollute** the wilderness environment...

Key:
X = error
👎 = missed opportunity

X   comma splicing
X   punctuation error
👎   new paragraph needed to introduce a new topic
X   common spelling errors
X   modal verb would add detail

Improved sample answer

    I think the pipeline would be the best **option. This** is because a lot of people would get jobs and the US states along the route would get more tax. It would also save the **United States** from having to import so much oil.

    I don't think that the **environmental** costs are a major **problem. The** Ogallala Aquifer does not appear to be a very important area for wildlife. The amount of carbon dioxide created might add to global warming but so far the changes to the climate have been small.

    However, drilling for oil in the Western **Arctic** Reserve is not a good option because the roads and drilling pads **would pollute** the wilderness environment...

Key:
✓ = correct use
👍 = improvement

✓   correct use of full stops to separate sentences
✓   capitals for place names
👍   indent shows start of new paragraph
✓   correct spelling
👍   modal verb **would** makes meaning clearer

Now try this

Look back at a piece of writing you have done for Geography recently.
(a) Check it three times: firstly for spelling mistakes, secondly for punctuation errors, and finally for grammatical sense. Aim to find at least five mistakes.
(b) Write out a corrected version. Can you find ways of making your sentence constructions more sophisticated too?

Improving answers: Religious Studies

This extract from a student's answer to a Religious Studies question contains a number of errors, as well as missed opportunities to score highly for SPaG. The improved response corrects the errors and adds impact by using more sophisticated SPaG techniques.

Worked example

'Religious believers should not eat meat.'
Do you agree? Give reasons for your answer, showing that you have thought about more than one point of view. Refer to religious arguments in your answer.   **(6 marks, plus 4 marks for SPAG)**

Response with errors

Both **buddhists** and **hindus** follow a **principal** known as ahimsa, **who** forbids harming living creatures. In fact, most **buddhists** are vegetarians because the Surangama Sutra says that living creatures should not be killed, treated violently or tormented.

Many people believe eating meat should be an individual **persons'** choice. They point to religious justifications for this. For example, Peter is told that no food is unclean and the **romans are written to by Paul** to say that all food may be eaten. Christians, **jews** and **muslims** believe that animals were created by God to provide humans with food. They believe it is **acceptible** to eat meat provided that food laws (kosher and halal) are obeyed...

Key:
X = error
👎 = missed opportunity

X   incorrect punctuation
X   incorrect homophone
X   incorrect relative pronoun
👎   adverbial would help
X   misplaced apostrophe
👎   clumsy passive clause
X   suffix spelling error

Improved sample answer

Both **Buddhists** and **Hindus** follow a **principle** known as ahimsa, **which** forbids harming living creatures. In fact, most **Buddhists** are vegetarians because the Surangama Sutra says that living creatures should not be killed, treated violently or tormented.

On the other hand, many people believe eating meat should be an individual **person's** choice. They point to religious justifications for this. For example, Peter is told that no food is unclean and **Paul writes to the Romans** to say that all food may be eaten. Christians, **Jews** and **Muslims** believe that animals were created by God to provide humans with food. They believe it is **acceptable** to eat meat provided that food laws (kosher and halal) are obeyed...

Key:
✓ = correct use
👍 = improvement

✓   correct capitalisation of religious groups
✓   correct homophone
✓   correct relative pronoun
👍   adverbial clearly introduces different opinion
✓   's added to a singular noun to indicate possession
✓   active clause sounds better here
✓   correct suffix spelling

Now try this

Look back at a piece of writing you have done for Religious Studies recently.

(a) Check it three times: firstly for spelling mistakes, secondly for punctuation errors and finally for grammatical sense. Aim to find at least five mistakes.

(b) Write out a corrected version. Can you find ways of making your sentence constructions more sophisticated too?

Improving answers: Biology

Although there are no SPaG marks allocated specifically for Biology, clear, correct writing will help you effectively express your reasoning in extended answers. This student's answer to a Biology question contains a number of errors, as well as missed opportunities for making the writing clearer.

Worked example

Some crops have been modified to produce a toxin when their cells are damaged. This toxin kills caterpillars when they eat the crop. Evaluate the factors that would need to be considered before growing these crops on a large scale.

(6 marks)

Response with errors

First, you would need to consider whether this method is effective at killing caterpillars and increasing the crop **yeild**. **Geneticly** modifying a crop can be *expensive*. **Tests** would need to be carried out to find out whether the increased **yeild** brings in enough income to offset the cost of buying the genetically modified seeds to **plant**. **You** would also need to know whether the toxin is **harmfull** to people eating the crop. Again, **people should do some tests** to make sure that the crop is safe to eat. **Its** important that consumers are happy to buy this crop.

Key:
X = error
👎 = missed opportunity

👎 colon would help
👎 new paragraph would help to introduce the new point
X common spelling errors
X missing apostrophe
👎 passive clause would be better here

Improved sample answer

First, you would need to consider whether this method is effective at killing caterpillars and increasing the crop **yield**. **Genetically** modifying a crop can be **expensive: tests** would need to be carried out to find out whether the increased **yield** brings in enough income to offset the cost of buying the genetically modified seeds to plant.

You would also need to know whether the toxin is **harmful** to people eating the crop. Again, **tests must be carried out** to make sure that the crop is safe to eat. **It's** important that consumers are happy to buy this crop.

Key:
✓ = correct use
👍 = improvement

👍 colon introduces further explanation
👍 indent clearly shows start of new paragraph
✓ correct spellings
✓ **it's** with an apostrophe means **it is**
👍 question uses the passive, so this passive clause is more appropriate

Now try this

Look back at a piece of writing you have done for Biology recently.
- **(a)** Check it three times: firstly for spelling mistakes, secondly for punctuation errors and finally for grammatical sense. Aim to find at least five mistakes.
- **(b)** Write out a corrected version. Can you find ways of making your sentence constructions more sophisticated too?

Improving answers: Chemistry

Although there are no SPaG marks allocated specifically for Chemistry, clear, correct writing will help you effectively express your reasoning in extended answers. This student's answer to a Chemistry question contains a number of errors, as well as missed opportunities for making the writing clearer.

Worked example

Soluble salts can be made by the reactions of acids with insoluble metal compounds. The salt produced depends on the reactants chosen. Devise a method to prepare pure, dry crystals of zinc sulfate, $ZnSO_4$, from a zinc compound and a suitable acid. Begin your answer by choosing suitable reactants. You should also write a balanced equation as part of your plan.

(6 marks)

Key:
✗ = error
👎 = missed opportunity

Response with errors

I would use zinc carbonate and sulfuric acid. **Equation for the reaction:**

ZNCO3 + H2SO4 → ZNSO4 + H2O + CO2

First, I would put some of the acid in a beaker and warm it with a **bunsen** burner, tripod and **gauze. I** would use a spatula to add a little zinc carbonate to the warm acid and stir it with a **stiring** rod. I would repeat until all the bubbling **stoped** and some solid was left in the bottom of the **beaker.** I would filter the mixture to remove the excess zinc carbonate, using a filter funnel and filter paper. I would collect the **zinck** sulfate solution in a conical flask.

👎 full sentence would be better
✗ missing lower-case letters and subscript numbers
👎 new paragraphs and conjunctions needed
✗ common spelling errors
✗ punctuation error
✗ incorrect spelling of key term

Improved sample answer

    I would use zinc carbonate and sulfuric acid. **This is the equation for the reaction:**

$ZnCO_3 + H_2SO_4 → ZnSO_4 + H_2O + CO_2$

First, I would put some of the acid in a beaker and warm it with a **Bunsen** burner, tripod and gauze.

    I would **then** use a spatula to add a little zinc carbonate to the warm acid and stir it with a **stirring** rod. I would repeat until all the bubbling **stopped** and some solid was left in the bottom of the beaker.

    Next, I would filter the mixture to remove the excess zinc carbonate, using a filter funnel and filter paper. I would collect the **zinc** sulfate solution in a conical flask.

Key:
✓ = correct use
👍 = improvement

👍 verb added to make a complete sentence
✓ correctly written according to scientific convention
👍 conjunctions and new paragraphs help, new paragraphs define order of actions
✓ correct suffixes added
✓ correct spelling
✓ correct spelling of key term

Now try this

Look back at a piece of writing you have done for Chemistry recently.

(a) Check it three times: firstly for spelling mistakes, secondly for punctuation errors and finally for grammatical sense. Aim to find at least five mistakes.

(b) Write out a corrected version. Can you find ways of making your sentence constructions more sophisticated too?

Improving answers: Physics

Although there are no SPaG marks allocated specifically for Physics, clear, correct writing will help you effectively express your reasoning in extended answers. This student's answer to a Physics question contains a number of errors, as well as missed opportunities for making the writing clearer.

Worked example

Unstable nuclei emit ionising radiation which can cause damage to human tissue. Explain the precautions that need to be taken in order to reduce the potential danger of ionising radiation to humans.

Your answer should refer to the nature of ionising radiation and how it may be dangerous both inside and outside the body.　　**(6 marks)**

Response with errors

Ionising radiation is radiation that has enough energy to **nock** electrons from the outer shells of atoms, turning them from neutral atoms to positively charged ions. There are three types of ionising radiation from the **nucleus alpha**, beta and gamma radiation. Alpha radiation is the **more** ionising and gamma-rays **were** the **less** ionising.

Since ionising radiation can damage human tissue and cause mutations in cells, leading to **cancer it was** necessary to take precautions. These precautions **include wearing** lead aprons to absorb the **radiation, being** exposed to as low a radiation energy as **possible, being** as far from the radioactive source as **possible and** being exposed for as short a period of time as possible.

Key:

✗ = error

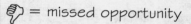 = missed opportunity

✗　common spelling error
✗　missing punctuation
✗　incorrect comparatives
✗　missing comma
✗　inconsistent use of tenses
👎　colons followed by semi-colons would be better here

Improved sample answer

　　　Ionising radiation is radiation that has enough energy to **knock** electrons from the outer shells of atoms, turning them from neutral atoms to positively charged ions. There are three types of ionising radiation from the **nucleus:** alpha, beta and gamma radiation. Alpha radiation is the **most** ionising and gamma-rays **are** the **least** ionising.

　　　Since ionising radiation can damage human tissue and cause mutations in cells, leading to **cancer, it is** necessary to take precautions. Precautions **include the following: wearing** lead aprons to absorb the **radiation;** **being** exposed to as low a radiation energy as **possible;** **being** as far from the radioactive source as **possible; and** being exposed for as short a period of time as possible.

Key:

✓ = correct use

👍 = improvement

✓　silent letter 'k' spelled correctly
✓　colon used before a phrase or explanation
✓　correct superlatives
✓　comma used to separate subordinate clause from main clause
✓　tense used consistently
👍　colon introduces series of clauses separated by semi-colons

Now try this

Look back at a piece of writing you have done for Physics recently.

(a) Check it three times: firstly for spelling mistakes, secondly for punctuation errors and finally for grammatical sense. Aim to find at least five mistakes.

(b) Write out a corrected version. Can you find ways of making your sentence constructions more sophisticated too?

Improving answers: English Literature

This extract from a student's answer to an English Literature question contains a number of errors, as well as missed opportunities to score highly for SPaG. The improved response corrects the errors and adds impact by using more accurate and sophisticated SPaG techniques.

Worked example

Discuss the theme of marriage in *Romeo and Juliet*.   **(40 marks, plus 4 SPaG marks)**

Response with errors

Shakespear shows how conflict can develop when, in **act 1**, Capulet **beleives** that Juliet is too young to marry since she is **yet a stranger in the world**. However, by Act 3 he is less **tolerent** when she refuses to marry Paris and he determines to "drag" her to church **on a hurdle** if she disobeys him. His comments reveal his changed attitude **and** highlight the position of women **and** the pressure on Elizabethan daughters to obey **there** fathers...

Key:
X = error
👎 = missed opportunity

X incorrect spelling of key word
X incorrect punctuation
X common spelling errors
X missing speech marks
👎 repetition of **and**

Improved sample answer

Shakespeare shows how conflict can develop when, in **Act 1**, Capulet **believes** that Juliet is too young to marry since she is **"yet a stranger in the world"**. However, by Act 3 he is less **tolerant** when she refuses to marry Paris and he determines to "drag" her to church **"on a hurdle"** if she disobeys him. His comments **not only** reveal his changed attitude **but also** highlight the position of women and the pressure on Elizabethan daughters to obey **their** fathers...

Key:
✓ = correct use
👍 = improvement

✓ correct spelling of key words
✓ capitals for titles
✓ common spelling mistakes checked and corrected
✓ speech marks used for direct quotation
👍 essay phrases make sentence construction more sophisticated

Now try this

Look back at a piece of writing you have done for English Literature recently.

(a) Check it three times: firstly for spelling mistakes, secondly for punctuation errors; and finally for grammatical sense. Aim to find at least five mistakes.

(b) Write out a corrected version. Can you find ways of making your sentence constructions more sophisticated too?

Improving answers: English Language

This extract from a student's answer to an English Language question contains a number of errors, as well as missed opportunities to score highly for SPaG. The improved response corrects the errors and adds impact by using more accurate and sophisticated SPaG techniques.

Worked example

'Teenagers do not contribute positively to society. All they do is cause trouble.'
Write an article for a national newspaper in which you explain your point of view on this statement.

(40 marks, plus 4 SPaG marks)

Response with errors

An regular reader of this **news-paper** may well feel that all teenagers **does** is hang around on street corners sipping bottles of alcohol and spitting at passers-by. Some readers may choose to **by** into the idea that all teenagers **is** trouble.
This image sells newspapers. **It is not the whole story.** Positive stories do exist. Some **teenager's don't make no** effort to contribute to society. However, I know of more teenagers who get it **write** than get it wrong. **52% of teenagers** at our local secondary school have received some form of award or prize...

Key:
✗ = error
👎 = missed opportunity

✗ incorrect article
✗ incorrect hyphen
✗ incorrect subject–verb agreement
👎 a rhetorical question would be better here
✗ unnecessary apostrophe
✗ double negative
✗ incorrect homophones
👎 an essay phrase would help here

Improved sample answer

A regular reader of this **newspaper** may well feel that all teenagers **do** is hang around on street corners sipping bottles of alcohol and spitting at passers-by. Some readers may choose to **buy** into the idea that all teenagers **are** trouble. This image sells newspapers. **But is it the whole story?** Positive stories do exist. Some **teenagers don't make any** effort to contribute to society. However, I know of more teenagers who get it **right** than get it wrong. **For example, 52% of teenagers** at our local secondary school have received some form of award or prize...

Key:
✓ = correct use
👍 = improvement

✓ correct article
✓ correct hyphenation
✓ subject–verb agreement
👍 rhetorical question draws reader in
✓ correct use of an apostrophe
✓ correct form of the negative
✓ correct homophones
👍 an essay phrase introduces statistic

Now try this

Look back at a piece of writing you have done for English Language recently.
(a) Check it three times: firstly for spelling mistakes, secondly for punctuation errors and finally for grammatical sense. Aim to find at least five mistakes.
(b) Write out a corrected version. Can you find ways of making your sentence constructions more sophisticated too?

Answers

ENGLISH FOR EXAMS

1. Standard English

(a) There is no excuse for ruining the environment for the children of the future.

(b) The main character of this novel doesn't seem to be a good man.

(c) Macbeth should not have killed his friend, King Duncan.

2. Formal & informal language

Suggested answers:

1 I would like to discuss further; I wish to proceed with; I find it unacceptable that.

2 Currently, it appears that the decision of the politicians will damage the economy.

SPELLING

3. Double letters

1 exp<u>or</u>t (but <u>ex</u>port when used as a noun); <u>travel</u>; com<u>plain</u>; el<u>ect</u>; <u>straighten</u>

2 permitted

3 jogged; opening; entered; admitted

4. Silent letters

1 salmon; rhythm; indi<u>c</u>tment; balle<u>t</u>; <u>w</u>rist

2 <u>k</u>not; <u>s</u>word; thum<u>b</u>; whis<u>t</u>le; ca<u>l</u>ves; <u>h</u>onour

3 ve<u>g</u>etables; <u>d</u>escription; calend<u>a</u>r; nec<u>e</u>ssary; <u>g</u>uesthouse

5. Plurals: adding -s and -es

1 processes; landscapes; knights; ecosystems; boxes; businesses; biases; dishes; minuses; complexes

2 eyelash; synonym; prospectus; quiz; phrase; fish; guide; church; mix; equinox

3 The pupils sat on the benches while the teachers sorted out their classes.

4 The painters put the brushes into the jars and examined the atlases and the sketches.

6. Plurals: words ending in -y

1

Vowel before -y	Consonant before -y
attorney; decoy; galley; holiday; survey	clergy; century; necessity; prophecy; deity

2

Vowel before -y	Consonant before -y
attorneys; decoys; galleys; holidays; surveys	clergies; centuries; necessities; prophecies; deities

7. Plurals: other endings

1 leaves; selves; debriefs; wolves; roofs

2 (a) The wives took some knives off the shelves and put them in the safes due to their beliefs about safety.

(b) I saw some elves on the roofs, running for their lives from some wolves.

8. Irregular plurals

1 His hypotheses were based on analyses of fish genera and observation of salmon in their natural habitat.

2 All people should chase the geese, sheep and oxen out of the three aircraft.

9. Prefixes

1 <u>dis</u>loyal; <u>im</u>perfection; <u>non</u>stop; <u>mal</u>nourished; <u>un</u>realistic; <u>il</u>literate; <u>in</u>compatible; <u>ir</u>reversible; <u>mis</u>diagnosis; <u>de</u>code; <u>ana</u>erobic

2 Answers will vary.

10. Suffixes: changes to word endings

1 (a) theories   (b) prayed   (c) envious
(d) securely   (e) tying

2 (a) beautiful   (b) dying   (c) approximately
(d) valleys   (e) studied

11. Suffixes: adding to root words

1 cre<u>ation</u>; neglig<u>ence</u>; absor<u>bent</u>; prevent<u>able</u>; mar<u>tial</u>; preten<u>tious</u>

2 Answers will vary.

12. Homophones: contractions

1 (a) Why is <u>there</u> so much traffic today?
(b) Germany was forced to pay reparations to <u>its</u> neighbours.
(c) Please call if you have not received <u>your</u> parcel.

2 (a) <u>There</u> is no evidence for <u>your</u> argument.
(b) The dog thinks <u>it's</u> time for <u>its</u> tea.
(c) <u>You're</u> not leaving the party before <u>it's</u> over.
(d) <u>It's</u> not right that <u>you're</u> covering up for <u>their</u> errors.

13. Homophones: common groups

1 (a) to
(b) allowed

2 (a) <u>Where</u> did Macbeth and Banquo meet the three <u>witches</u>?
(b) She <u>passed</u> her driving test and now she has her <u>licence</u>.
(c) In <u>which</u> room can I <u>practise</u> reading my <u>two</u> speeches <u>aloud</u>?

14. Common spelling errors

(a) On your <u>advice</u>, I <u>bought</u> a watch <u>off</u> the internet. I hope I won't <u>lose</u> it.

(b) A lot <u>of</u> <u>our</u> employees are expressing their <u>dissent</u> in the streets.

(c) Engineers have made a <u>thorough</u> examination of the <u>device</u> and they <u>advise</u> that it is now safe.

(d) Even <u>though</u> the room was <u>quiet</u>, everyone was awake <u>except</u> George.

15. 'i' before 'e'
1 thi<u>e</u>f; rec<u>ei</u>ve; fi<u>e</u>ld; decaff<u>ei</u>nated; conc<u>ei</u>ve
2 beli<u>e</u>f; n<u>ei</u>ghbour; dec<u>ei</u>tful; b<u>ei</u>ge; pri<u>e</u>st; fi<u>e</u>rce; l<u>ei</u>sure

16. Spellings for GCSE History
Answers will vary, depending on the words you find difficult to spell.

17. Spellings for GCSE Geography
Answers will vary, depending on the words you find difficult to spell.

18. Spellings for GCSE Religious Studies
Answers will vary, depending on the words you find difficult to spell.

19. Spellings for GCSE Biology
Answers will vary, depending on the words you find difficult to spell.

20. Spellings for GCSE Chemistry
Answers will vary, depending on the words you find difficult to spell.

21. Spellings for GCSE Physics
Answers will vary, depending on the words you find difficult to spell.

22. Spellings for GCSE English Literature
Answers will vary, depending on the words you find difficult to spell.

23. Spellings for GCSE English Language
Answers will vary, depending on the words you find difficult to spell.

PUNCTUATION

24. Capital letters
(a) Joseph Smith founded the Church of Latter-Day Saints, whose followers are known as Mormons.
(b) On the first Wednesday after Easter, I have my German exam in Berlin.
(c) The North Atlantic Treaty Organisation was founded in 1949 in Washington, but its headquarters are in Belgium.

25. Sentence endings
(a) I think Curley is a menacing character, don't you?
(b) The narrator says, "But debt is a debt and must be paid."
(c) It was Mark Twain who said, "One should never use exclamation points in writing. It is like laughing at your own jokes."
(d) What an incredibly stupid thing to do!

26. Commas for extra information
(a) Because commuters go to work early and return late, commuter towns can seem deserted during the day.

(b) Odo and his brother, whose name was Robert of Mortain, took refuge in Pevensey Castle.
(c) With over a billion followers, Islam is the world's second largest religion.

27. Commas in lists
(a) Hard engineering methods for managing floods include building embankments, flood walls, reservoirs and flood barriers.
(b) The feudal hierarchy consisted of the King, his tenants-in-chief, their under-tenants and the peasants.
(c) Macbeth is a fearless, ambitious nobleman. The Three Witches are strange, deceitful and untrustworthy. The porter is a comic minor character.

28. Avoiding comma splicing
Suggested answers:
(a) They wanted to go for a walk, so they put on their walking boots.
(b) "All animals are equal, but some animals are more equal than others."
(c) William invaded in the south; Harold was fighting in the north.

29. Avoiding other comma errors
1 (a) Thomas Hardy wrote about life in Wessex, which is a historical county.
　(b) Sigmund Freud, an Austrian neurologist, developed a theory that humans have an unconscious.
2 (a) Spits are narrow projections of sand or shingle <u>that</u> are attached to the land at one end.
　(b) Andheri railway station, <u>which</u> is one of the busiest stations in the world, is in a popular suburb of Mumbai.

30. Colons
(a) There was only one thing to do: join the revolution!
(b) I need you to find these things for me: a knife, some tape and a plastic bottle.
(c) A flow map has a clear advantage over others: it shows direction and volume of movement.
(d) Italian is quite easy to pronounce: most words end with a vowel.

31. Semi-colons
(a) We need the following items: a large table with sturdy legs; a map of Manchester, England; and two cans of paint, which should preferably be green.
(b) The author was finally published in 2017; she had worked for years on her novel.

2. Brackets and dashes

Eating a healthier diet (lower fat, sugar and salt) can be used to treat cardiovascular disease.

The economy of the United States – the largest in the world in terms of GDP – is approximately a quarter of gross world product.

3. Hyphens

Barack Obama is now an ex-president and a former commander-in-chief.

Their new pet was an extremely enthusiastic, accident-prone, three-month-old puppy.

4. Speech marks

(a) The general ordered, "Move the cavalry into position."

(b) "I write for six hours every day," replied the author.

(c) "Why are you so scared?" asked the girl with the long hair.

(d) "We don't have a cat," he admitted, "but we do have three dogs."

(e) "No surrender!" shouted the protestor.

5. Contractions

didn't; should've; we'll; isn't; weren't

I'm; she could've; you mightn't; who'll; that'd

they will not; what are; we have; how is or how has; you cannot (or you can not)

6. Possession: singular

(a) a monk's vows

(b) Angus's personality

(c) a biome's climate

(d) Nikita Khrushchev's leadership

(a) the investigation's results

(b) the article's tone

(c) Islam's doctrines

(d) the deceased man's possessions

(e) the coast's geology

7. Possession: plural

the dogs' bones; the children's toys; a women's scarf; the characters' motivations; the bacteria's influence

The armies' defeat was blamed on the men's lack of experience.

GRAMMAR

8. Articles

(a) An effective way to book a hotel is to use one of those price comparison sites.

(b) It was an honour to receive such a lot of fan mail from a European country.

9. Different types of pronoun

Lead is a dense, soft metal. It is non-corroding but toxic. Its atomic number is 82. The Romans used it for making their water pipes and lining their baths.

2 The relative pronoun is **bold** and the relative clause is underlined here:

In 2013, Pope Benedict XVI, **whose** real name was Joseph Ratzinger, was the first pope to resign since 1415.

40. Using pronouns

(a) Please would you email it to me?

(b) Suzie and I made a discovery.

(c) The examiner was very rude to my brother and me.

(d) I gave myself a pat on the back.

41. Less or fewer? Who or whom?

1 less distress; fewer mistakes; less woodland; fewer abbots; less biodiversity; less than a century; less than two million pounds; fewer than six deities; less than 25 miles; fewer bacteria

2 (a) James II, who was deposed in the Glorious Revolution, died in 1633.

(b) With whom are you going to the cinema?

(c) The scientist whom we met yesterday just won a prize.

(d) The papers blamed the politicians, several of whom have now resigned.

42. Whose or who's? That or which?

(a) The politicians whose policies led to the problems have escaped any blame.

(b) The effects of climate change, which are already being felt around the world, may soon become more intense.

(c) Christian practices that people observe in their own homes include praying and Bible reading.

(d) The research scientist, who's made an exciting discovery, does not want to be interviewed.

43. Have or of? Effect or affect?

1 (a) The increasing population is likely to affect local services.

(b) The increasing population will have a significant effect on local services.

2 (a) By 2050, the number of Muslims may have equalled the number of Christians around the world.

(b) Napoleon could have won the Battle of Waterloo but he underestimated the enemy.

(c) I should have realised my mistake, then I might have been able to do something about it.

44. Negatives

Chapter 4 shows that the character doesn't really have any close friends. He isn't very good in social situations. He doesn't know anybody in his class. He thinks it isn't fair that he hasn't got anyone to rely on.

45. Active and passive

1 (a) The Jews were persecuted (passive)

(b) His sister had been raised in an orphanage (passive)

(c) The ecosystem had recovered from the pollution (active)

(d) An adverb can be used to modify a verb (passive)

(e) The soldier fought by himself against the enemy forces (active)

2 Shilpa knocked over the lamp.

46. Simple present tense

1 (a) he lies   (b) she goes   (c) he washes
   (d) she buries   (e) it fixes

2 I am; you run; he goes; she does; it mixes; he plays; she bullies; it fizzes; we stand; they swim

47. Present continuous tense

sleeping; marvelling; having; cancelling; planning; entering; enjoying; dying; frolicking; living; inferring

48. Simple past tense

hosted; equalled; cancelled; outlined; studied; admitted; visited; tidied; stopped; followed

49. Irregular past tense

The day of the battle began with a bad decision. The general spoke to his advisors and chose to place his cavalry far in the rear. However, he hadn't thought about the poor weather: it had been raining for days. If he had known that the horses would struggle in the mud, then the enemy might not have broken through and stolen victory.

50. The future

(a) The prisoner will escape from prison and (will) make his way home.

(b) My friend leaves by train in the morning.

(c) The particle physicist is going to reveal her discovery to the world.

(d) My secondary school class is having a reunion this year.

51. Modal verbs

1 (a) The rumours may (possibility) be true but I couldn't (ability) tell you where they came from.

   (b) You ought to (necessity) go soon or you could (possibility) miss your train.

2 Answers may vary. Suggested answers:

   (a) "This will end badly," she sighed.

   (b) Pollution can cause acid rain.

   (c) You must wear safety goggles.

52. Subject–verb agreement

(a) The keys to the door and the vault are missing.

(b) My team practises every day after school.

(c) Each of these sentences includes a gap to fill.

(d) Some chemicals and biological agents are extremely toxic.

(e) The military police have arrested the fugitive soldier.

53. Tense consistency

1 Magnesium is a silvery-white metal. It ignites easily in air and burns with a bright light. It is an essential element to life but it does not occur uncombined in nature.

2 In 1204, an army of about 20,000 soldiers broke into the city of Constantinople. This army of the Fourth Crusade looted, pillaged and slaughtered its way through the great city.

STRUCTURING WRITING

54. Paragraphs

Time, Person, Topic, Place. It reminds me to start a new paragraph when there is a change in time, person, topic or place.

55. Introductions

Answers will vary.

56. Conclusions

Answers will vary.

57. Conjunctions

1 In 1893, New Zealand was the first country to grant voting rights to women. Subsequently, other countries followed, although many only granted limited rights. When World War I began, women took on roles and jobs traditionally done by men. For example, they worked as railway guards, firefighters and bank clerks. As a result, the suffrage movement gained further momentum. However, it took until 1928 for women to be granted full voting rights in Britain.

2 Answers will vary.

58. Useful essay phrases

In order to understand the importance of the Qur'an in Islam, you must recognise that Muslims believe it is a sacred 'received' text. That is to say, they not only believe the words were revealed to the Prophet Mohammed directly by Allah but also believe those words have not been altered since. This means that Islamic people view the Qur'an as the ultimate source of guidance and treat it with reverence. For these reasons, Muslims do not speak, eat or drink when someone is reading the Qur'an.

59. Comparisons

1 older; larger; thinner; more peaceful; easier; more unusual; sadder; angrier; narrower; more generous

2 oldest; largest; thinnest; most peaceful; easiest; most unusual; saddest; angriest; narrowest; most generous

60. Clauses

1 The subject is underlined and the verb is **bold** here:
   (a) The world population **reached** 7 billion in 2011.

(b) Every year, <u>most major cities</u> **hold** public marathons.

2 **(a)** <u>Although it has a cell wall</u>, a bacterial cell is not a type of plant cell. (subordinate clause)

(b) Normans believed in making acts of penance, <u>which included building churches or giving gifts to the Church</u>, to make up for the violence. (relative clause)

61. Simple sentences

(a) <u>Waltheof</u> (S) <u>informed</u> (V) <u>Archbishop Lefranc</u> (O) about the revolt.

(b) <u>Clip</u> (V) <u>the slide</u> (O) securely onto the stage. (The subject here is <u>you</u> – not included in an imperative (command) sentence.)

(c) <u>Mitosis</u> (S) <u>is</u> (V) <u>a type of cell division</u> (O).

(d) <u>Effective writing</u> (S) <u>uses</u> (V) <u>a variety of sentence types</u> (O).

(e) <u>Was</u> (V) <u>this</u> (S) <u>the end of Anglo-Saxon resistance</u> (O)?

62. Compound sentences

(a) Most scientists agree that the Earth's climate is warming <u>yet/but</u> a few deny it may be caused by human activity.

(b) Siddhartha Gautama was shocked by the suffering he witnessed outside his palace <u>so</u> he left his life of luxury to search for answers.

63. Complex sentences

1 The subordinate clauses are underlined and the main clauses are bold here:

(a) Christian meetings were dangerous <u>because the Romans persecuted them</u>.

(b) <u>If a population was allowed to grow too much</u>, **famine would result**, <u>which would reduce the population size</u>.

2 **(a)** Aluminium oxide is dissolved in molten cryolite, which reduces the temperature needed for electrolysis.

(b) When I heard the news, I dropped my phone in surprise.

64. Using quotations

Answers will vary.

65. Synonyms

Suggested answer – other answers are also possible:
In some countries, many people now live in megacities. A megacity has at least 10 million <u>inhabitants</u>. <u>Workers</u> are drawn to such cities from urban areas hoping for greater opportunities. This can have a negative effect on the <u>communities</u> left behind. Megacities are growing fast. For example, Mumbai's <u>population</u> doubled between 1991 and 2013.

EXAM SKILLS

66. Checking your work

1 There are 14 mistakes:
Having <u>too</u> lords would <u>of</u> been difficult for <u>them</u> barons with lands in both <u>normandy</u> and <u>england</u>. <u>indeed</u>, many of the <u>importantest</u> barons <u>was</u> in this <u>postion</u>. These nobles would <u>of</u> had to deal with <u>to</u> different administrations, two tax systems and two <u>diffrent</u> systems of <u>militry obligations</u>

2 Having <u>two</u> lords would <u>have</u> been difficult for <u>those</u> barons with lands in both <u>Normandy</u> and <u>England</u>. <u>Indeed</u>, many of the <u>most important</u> barons <u>were</u> in this <u>position</u>. These nobles would <u>have</u> had to deal with <u>two</u> different administrations, two tax systems and two <u>different</u> systems of <u>military obligations</u>.

67. Correcting errors

(a) The Domesday Book is a̶ ̶n̶o̶t̶h̶e̶r̶ ̶e̶x̶a̶m̶p̶e̶l̶ [another example] of k̶i̶n̶g̶ [King] William's w̶i̶l̶l̶i̶a̶m̶s̶'̶ growing power over ʌhis conquered kingdom.

(b) Satellites are y̶o̶u̶s̶e̶d̶ [used] ʌ to spot tropical cyclones and to track t̶h̶e̶r̶e̶ ̶p̶r̶o̶g̶r̶e̶s̶ [their progress].

(c) Starting a piece ʌof writing can ʌbe difficult. You need to ʌgrab the r̶e̶a̶d̶e̶r̶s̶ [reader's] attention.

68–75. Improving answers

Answers will vary.

Notes

Notes

Notes

Notes

Published by Pearson Education Limited, 80 Strand, London, WC2R 0RL.

www.pearsonschoolsandfecolleges.co.uk

Text © Pearson Education Limited 2017
Edited, typeset and produced by Elektra Media Ltd
Original illustrations © Pearson Education Limited 2017
Illustrated by Elektra Media Ltd
Cover illustration by Eoin Coveney

The right of Giles Clare to be identified as author of this work has been asserted by him in accordance with the Copyright, Designs and Patents Act 1988.

First published 2017

20 19 18 17
10 9 8 7 6 5 4 3 2 1

British Library Cataloguing in Publication Data
A catalogue record for this book is available from the British Library

ISBN 9781292211527

Printed in Slovakia by Neografia.

We would like to thank the following authors of other Pearson titles for some of the subject-specific example content featured in this title: Jonathan Morgan, Julie Hughes, David Grant, Rob Bircher, Michael Chiles, Mike O'Neill, Nigel Saunders, Pauline Lowrie, Susan Kearsey and Kirsty Taylor.